Hungarian

4 IN 1

Main courses

Hungarian soups

Cold & Hot sauces

Salads, Pasta salads & Sweet pastas

The most popular recipes step by step!

J. S. JOZEF

BOOK 1

Main courses

BOOK 2

Hungarian soups

BOOK 3

Cookbook for beginners

Cold & Hot sauces

BOOK 4

Salads, Pasta salads

&

Sweet pastas

Table of contens

Copyright © 2018. All Rights Reserved. 3

BOOK 1...................20

1. Chicken roast.......................22

Noodles.................................24

2. Stuffed cabbage.....................25

3. Beef stew 28

4. Mushroom stew 31

5. Potato casserole with eggs and sausages.................................33

6. Stuffed pepper.....................35

7. Potatoes with paprika...........37

8. Meat pasta 39

9. Roast a la Brasov 41

10. Hunter's stew 43

11. Pea stew 45

12. Rice with meat....................47

13. Lentils stew.........................49

14. Meatballs 51

15. Hungarian ratatouille 52

16. Stuffed chicken thigh 54

17. Plum dumpling....................56

18. Kebab skewer 58

19. Boiled hand of pork.............60

20. Bean salad 62

21. Goose liver served in its fat ..63

22. Swedish mushroom salad.....65

23. Lentils salad with gamey meat
....67

24. Aspic chicken stew 69

25. Crab salad a la Zala 71

26. Potato ganca........................72

27. Shepherd meat 74

28. Cholent with smoked pork loin
....75

29. With kidney marrow 78

30. Pike with beans....................79

31. Serbian carp.........................81

32. Székely catfish ragout 83

33. Shepherd boy's roast 85

34. Fried calf leg 87

35. Roast a la Csáki 88

36. Pork leg a la Pékné 91

37. Roast a la Göcsej 93

38. Butcher's stew 95

39. Rooster testicle stew...........96

BOOK 2..................................98

Vegetables: 103

1. Potato soup with bacon 107

2. Cheese cream soup in bread 109

3. Meatball soup.....................112

4. Bean goulash 114

5. Tomato soup 116

6. Pumpkin cream soup 118

7. Garlic cream soup 121

8. Fisherman's soup a la Baja ...123

9. Broth 125

10. Semolina noodle soup........128

11. Fruit soup 131

12. Frankfurter soup 133

13. Palóc soup 135

14. Korhely soup.....................137

15. Chicken soup a la Újház......139

16. Green bean soup...............141

17. Fried soup.........................142

18. Egg soup with cumin 144

19. Dill soup 145

20. Celery cream soup 147

21. Quince soup 148

22. Lebbencs soup 150

23. Cauliflower soup 152

24. Outlaw soup a la Bakony....155

25. Beetroot soup 157

26. Plum soup.........................159

27. Meatball soup with snail dough.................................161

28. Diet celery soup 163

29. Diet pear soup 165

30. Broccoli cream soup with toasted almond 167

BOOK 3...................................169

1 Mayonnaise sauce 172

Ingredients:............................172

2 Tartar sauce.........................173

3 Remoulade sauce..................175

4 Cream sauce 177

....178

5 Green sauce.........................178

6 Tyrol sauce 180

7 Moscow sauce 182

8 Gibice sauce.........................183

9 Swedish sauce 185

10 Csiki sauce 187

11 Chives sauce 188

12 Green chaud-froid sauce 190

13 Apple horseradish sauce 191

14 Cumberland sauce 193

15 Dutch sauce 194

16 Curry sauce 195

17 White sauce 197

.... 198

18 Malta sauce 198

19 Mustard sauce 200

20 Tomato sauce with mustard 201

21 Dutch sauce 203

22 Charon sauce 204

23 Csiki sauce 205

24 Spring sauce....................... 207

25 Vinaigrette sauce 209

1 Sour cherry sauce 211

2 Apple sauce 212

3 Black pepper sauce 213

4 Dill sauce 215

5 Carrot sauce 216

6 Provance sauce 218

7 Sorrel sauce 219

8 Vegetable sauce....................221

9 Mushroom sauce 222

10 Hungarian sauce 224

11 Sausage sauce....................225

12 Metaxa sauce 226

13 Provanse sauce 228

14 Madeira sauce 229

15 Béchamel sauce 231

16 Spicy sauce 233

17 Horseradish sauce..............235

18 Sour cream and cheese sauce
.................................236

19 Sardine sauce......................238

20 Parade sauce 239

21 Black pepper sauce 241

22 Chakala sauce 242

23 Bread roll sauce with chicken
....244

24 Horseradish sauce with orange
....246

25 Dill sauce with sour cream ..248

26 Pizza sauce.........................249

BOOK 4....................................251

1 Lettuce salad 254

2 Boiled salad 256

3 Cucumber salad 257

4 Pepper salad.........................259

5 Tomato salad 260

6 Onion salad 262

7 Cabbage salad.......................263

8 Beetroot salad 264

9 Potato salad 266

10 Green bean salad 268

11 Broccoli salad......................269

Pasta salads....................271

1 Pasta salad with ham...........271

2 Pasta salad with sausage and corn.......................................273

3 Pasta salad with chicken breast 275

4 Pasta salad with smoked cheese 277

5 Pasta salad with Mediterranean tuna 279

6 Pasta salad with tuna and mayonnaise...............................281

7 Avocado pasta salad 283

8 Spaghetti salad 284

9 Rich pasta salad 286

10 Pasta salad with ham, cheese and pumpkin 288

Mayonnaise salads 290

1 French salad 290

2 Mayonnaise potato salad......291

3 Russian meat salad 293

4 Mayonnaise mushroom salad294

5 Mayonnaise cauliflower salad
....296

6 Mayonnaise herring salad 297

7 Mayonnaise mixed salad.......299

8 Mayonnaise green bean salad
....301

9 Mayonnaise pea salad 302

10 Pasta salad with yoghurt.....303

11 Pasta salad with chicken 306

12 Sweet potato salad with
chicken......................................308

Sweet pastas.....................309

1 Sweet noodle cake................309

2 Sweet cake with rice pudding311

3 Pasta boiled in milk...............312

4 Pasta made from wheat meal314

5 Cottage cheese dumpling......315

6 Ham cube 317

8 Meaty bag 320

9 Strapacka............................322

10 Light sweet noodle cake......323

11 Pasta with walnut and jam..326

12 Pasta with poppy seeds.......328

13 Baked pasta with apple and cinnamon 330

14 Tyrol cubes 332

15 Cherry strudel 334

BOOK 1
Main courses

Foreword

I don't know where to begin. I married a girl cook in 1981 whom I've been married to all these years. I was curious for every meal she made. I'm very picky, so she didn't have an easy job, but she manages to surprise me with delicious meals even today. This book praises her excellence, I'm merely its writer. I will share 39 delicious and cheap recipes.

Description

The Hungarian cuisine includes delicious meals that are full of flavor due to the variety of spices.

You will find that the main courses are the most important in the Hungarian cuisine, they are usually served with pasta, potato or rice. The most important ingredient for many of these dishes is the famous Hungarian pepper.

Not many know the taste of traditional Hungarian meals since Hungarian meals are not as widespread as others are.

This is another reason to check out the excellent Hungarian soups as this is the perfect surprise for your family, friends and guests.

Beginner and advanced cooks can learn these easy to made, wonderful recipes. Discover the secrets of the Hungarian cuisine!

What do you get?

I will share these special recipes from this country of 10 million. Every meal is interesting. What's also worth noting is that every meal contains meat. I will show you how to prepare these specialities!

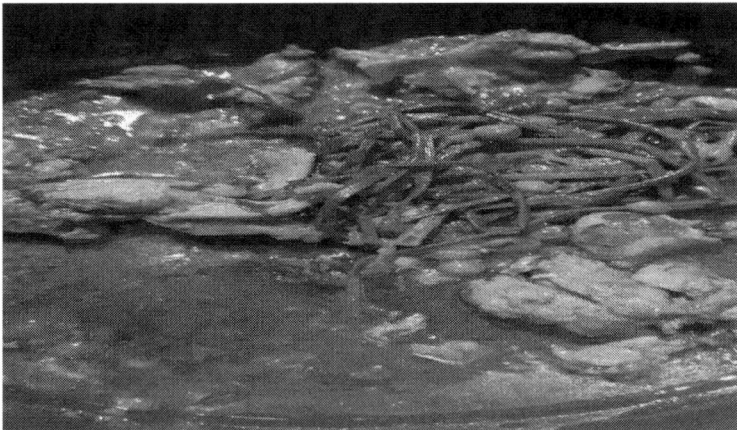

1. Chicken roast

Ingredients:

- 1 chicken
- 2 onions
- Red pepper

- Cooking oil
- Salt
- Ground black pepper
- 1 strong, green hot pepper

Preparation:

I slice up the chicken and wash it well. I peel the onions, cut them into small cubes and toast them on some oil.

I slice the hot pepper into small cubes as well, and toast them together, then add some red pepper and a bit of water. I put the sliced chicken into it, then add some salt and ground black pepper.

Cook it slowly until the meat is soft. You can add one spoon of flour mixed with cream, and once they are boiled, the chicken paprikash is ready.

Enjoy your meal! I recommend noodles as a side dis

Noodles

Ingredients:

- 500 g wheat flour
- 500 g pastry flour
- salt
- one egg

Preparation:

Mix the flour with the egg and add some salt. Make some pasta.

Boil some water and add a spoon of salt. Once it's boiling, add some dumplings into it. Mix it with a wooden spoon to keep the dumplings separated.

Cool it down with cold water, add some cooking oil and salt.

2. Stuffed cabbage

Ingredients:

- 1 smaller cabbage
- 1000 g sour cabbage
- 5-6 bay leaves
- Dry bread
- Whole black pepper

Stuffing:

- 1000 g minced meat
- 1 spoon of fat
- Salt
- Red pepper
- Ground black pepper
- Ground cumin
- 5 cloves of pressed garlic
- 200 g rice

Preparing the head of the cabbage:

I cut out the center of the cabbage, then boil it in salted water until the cabbage leaves get separated.

While they're boiling, I remove the leaves and put them on a tray. Once it's cooled, I cut out the thick parts and put the leaves into a bowl.

I pour some warm salted water onto it. Add some bay leaves, cumin, whole black pepper, then put dried bread on top, then close the lid. I leave it in a warm place for about a week until it gets sour. You can buy the sour cabbage heads in shops, however, this is tradition and it tastes even better!

Preparing the stuffing:

Put the minced meat into a bowl, add some fat if the meat is dry. Put in the spices; salt, red pepper, ground cumin, ground black pepper, 5 cloves of pressed garlic and mix them together.

Add the washed rice and we're done. Let it rest for a bit. Wash the sour cabbage if it is really sour. Twist it well so that it drains the water.

Stuff the cabbage heads, twist it and fold in its two ends. I lay out a kg of sour cabbage heads into a bowl, put the stuffed cabbages onto them, then put the rest of the small cabbage on top.

You can put smoked sausage or ham on top. Add some water, boil it, then boil the rice and cabbage heads until they are soft. Serve it with sour cream.

3. Beef stew

Ingredients:

- 1000 g of beef thighs and calves cut into cubes
- 2 onions
- 0.5 liters of red wine

- Some salt
- Ground black pepper
- Ground cumin
- Spice *(All spice?)*
- 1 white pepper
- 1 hot green pepper
- Ground red pepper – *Paprika*
- 5-6 bay leaves

Preparation:

Cut the meat into cubes and wash it, then cut the onions into cubes as well. Toast the onions on a bit of oil, then add the pepper cubes as well.

Once toasted, pour the red pepper on top, pour some water onto the meat, add some spices and boil it. Once it's soft, pour some red wine and boil it some more. Serve it with salted potatoes as a side dish.

Salted potatoes

Ingredients:

- 1000 g of potatoes
- Salt
- Water

Preparation:

Peel it, cut it into cubes, then wash the potatoes. Boil it in salted water until it's soft, then filter the water.

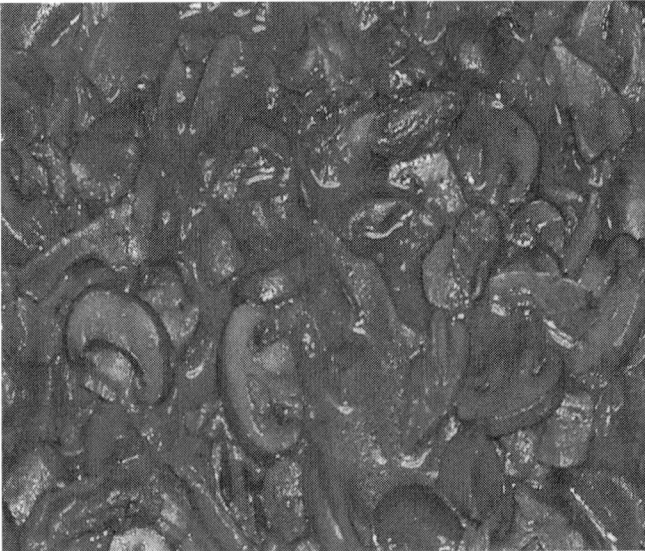

4. Mushroom stew

Ingredients:

- 1000 g agaricus mushroom
- 1 onion cut into cubes
- 1 white pepper cut into cubes
- Salt
- Ground black pepper
- Ground red pepper – Paprika
- Cooking oil
- 1 teaspoon of flour
- 1 small bottle of sour cream

Preparation:

Toast the onions in oil, add the white pepper cubes and continue toasting it, add some ground red pepper, pour water into it, then add some salt and black pepper. Put the sliced mushrooms into the bowl and boil until it's soft.

While the mushrooms are boiling, mix one spoon of flour with one small bottle of sour cream, then pour this into the bowl.

The mushroom stew is ready. Serve it with noodles, add some more black and hot pepper.

5. Potato casserole with eggs and sausages

Ingredients:

- 1000 g of potatoes
- 500 g of Vienna sausage
- 500 g of smoked sausage
- 1 big bottle of sour cream
- 10 eggs

Preparation:

Boil the potatoes in salted water until they are soft.

Boil the eggs for 15 minutes in salted water, and then toast the sausages and Vienna sausages in some oil.

I peel the boiled potatoes, then cut them in circles. I put oil into a medium sized oven pan, then I put half of the potatoes into it, put sliced sausages and Vienna sausages into it, then the sliced eggs, and finally cover the mix with the rest of the potatoes. I let it rest for a while then prepare the Béchamel sauce.

Béchamel sauce:

Ingredients:

- 200 g of flour
- 1 teaspoon of oil
- 1 egg
- 2 dl of milk

Preparation:

Prepare Béchamel sauce from 200 g of flour, toast the flour until it has the color of sand, then add one egg with milk and sour cream, add some salt and black pepper as well. Mix it together, pour it onto the potatoes, and bake it in a preheated

oven. Cut it into small cubes once done, and serve it with sour cream.

6. Stuffed pepper

Ingredients:

- 10 pieces of white pepper with seeds cut out
- 1kg of minced meat

- 200 g of rice
- Salt
- Black pepper
- 3 cloves of garlic
- 1 spoon of fat
- 1 egg
- 1 tablespoon Ground red pepper – *Paprika*
- 1 celery leaf
- 0.5 liter of tomato puree
- 2 onions
- Some oil
- 200 g of flour

Preparation:

Mix the minced meat with spices, fat, egg, pressed garlic.

Stuff the pepper with this mixture, boil the tomato puree, then add some onions, celery leaf and some water. Put the stuffed pepper into it so that it's submerged in water.

Add some salt. Boil it until it's soft. Fry it with salt and fat once the dumplings are ready. Fry it with

salt then add some sugar. The sauce should be light. You can serve it with boiled potatoes as well.

7. Potatoes with paprika

Ingredients:

- 1000 g of potatoes
- 300 g of smoked sausage

- 1 onion
- 3 cloves of garlic
- Salt
- Black pepper
- 1 spoon of fat
- 1 spoon of red pepper – Paprika
- Ground cumin
- Marjoram

Preparation:

Toast the onion cubes, then pour the red pepper onto it, put it into a bowl with some water and sliced sausages, then pour some more water so that it's submerged.

Put spices in there, and boil until soft.

You can add some pasta or egg barley. Serve it with sour or fresh bread.

8. Meat pasta

Ingredients:

- 1 package of small seashell shaped pasta
- 1000 g of minced meat
- 1 spoon of fat
- 1 onion
- 200 g of mushrooms
- 200 g of grated cheese
- 2 dl of tomato puree

- Salt
- Ground black pepper
- Rosemary
- Thyme

Preparation:

Cut the onion into cubes then toast it, add some minced meat with sliced mushrooms, toast it some more with spices, then pour the tomato puree onto it and cook until soft. While it's boiling, cook the pasta. Once we're done, mix them together. Pour it onto a pre-oiled oven pan, pour the grated cheese onto it and bake it in the oven. Once done, cut them into smaller slices and serve it with ketchup.

9. Roast a la Brasov

Ingredients:

- 1000 g of potatoes
- 1000 g of pork thighs
- 6 cloves of garlic
- Salt
- Black pepper
- Ground cumin
- Some tomato puree
- 1 spoon of oil
- Spices

- 1 spoon of flour

Preparation:

Slice the meat into small cubes, add some salt and black pepper, boil it under a lid. Add lots of water. Prepare the sauce.

Toast the flour on oil, then add some tomato puree. Once done, pour some more water on it and add spices.

The sauce should be thick!

Pour the sauce onto the meat and boil it. Add the pressed garlic towards the end. Cook the potato cubes in hot oil, then serve them together.

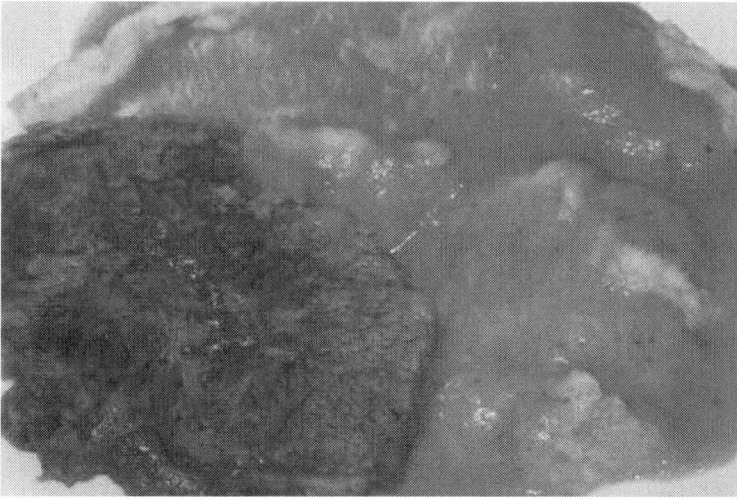

10. Hunter's stew

Ingredients:

- 1000 g of beef
- 300 g of vegetables
- 200 g of carrot
- Salt
- Black pepper
- 2 onions

- 3 pieces of bay leaves
- Mustard
- Some sugar
- 1 bottle of sour cream
- 1 package of macaroni pasta

Preparation:

Cook the peeled, finely cut vegetables with salt, bay leaves and black pepper, then put in the beef and boil it with enough water so that it is submerged. Once the vegetables are soft ground them into a puree, then prepare the sauce.

Toast a teaspoon of sugar in a bit of fat until it's caramelized, then pour water onto it. This gives the sauce a nice, brown look. Boil it with salt, mustard and sour cream and we're done with the sauce. If the beef is not soft enough, then boil it in some broth, and once it's cool, serve it sliced with the pasta.

11. Pea stew

Ingredients:

- 50 g of potatoes
- 2 medium onions
- 1 green pepper
- Cooking oil
- Salt
- 40 g of red pepper
- 1000 g of green peas

Preparation:

Slice up the onion. Toast it on a bit of oil, slice up the white pepper and toast them together.

Add some red pepper, salt and a bit of water. Put the peas in it, boil them until soft. We slice up the potatoes into circles and boil them together, spice it up with black pepper.

Noodles:

Ingredients:

- 1000 g pastry flour
- Salt
- Some water

Preparation:

Boil the water in a big bowl, add a spoon of salt, and once the water is boiling, add the noodles. Noodle dough should be semi hard, stir it while boiling, once done, filter it and pour water on top. Add some cooking oil so they don't get stuck. Enjoy your meal!

12. Rice with meat

Ingredients:

- 1000 g of pork thighs sliced up into cubes
- 2 onions
- 2 pepper
- Salt
- Black pepper
- Red pepper
- 50 g of rice

Preparation:

Slice up the onion into cubes, toast it on a bit of oil. Then add the sliced up pepper and red pepper, then some water, and boil it.

You can add some more salt or black pepper while it's boiling. Toast the rice on a bit of oil, then pour water onto it and boil it.

When done, pour it into the peas and boil until they are soft. Enjoy your meal!

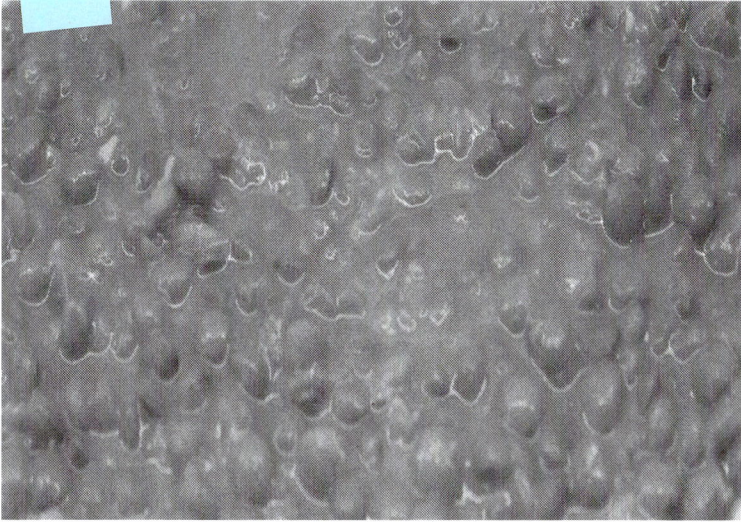

13. Lentils stew

Ingredients:

- 50 g of lentils
- 3 cloves of garlic
- 2 bay leaves
- Some mustard

- Salt
- Cukor
- Vinegar
- 200 g of flour
- Some oil
- 1 bottle of sour cream
- 0.5 liter of milk

Preparation:

Wash the lentils and boil it in water. Add some bay leaves, salt and pressed garlic.

Meanwhile, toast some flour on a bit of oil, then add the sour cream and milk. Pour this into the stew.

Add some mustard, vinegar, a bit of sugar and salt and boil them together.

14. Meatballs

Ingredients:

- 1000 g minced beef thighs
- 4 rolls
- Salt
- Black pepper
- Cumin
- 4 cloves of garlic
- Some red pepper

Preparation:

Soak the rolls then squeeze out the water, add some minced meat and spices, then mix them together with the rolls, add one egg as well. Make medium sized meatballs and fry it on oil.

15. Hungarian ratatouille

Ingredients:

- 1000 g of peppers
- 50 g of tomatoes
- 3 onions
- Some oil
- 200 g of bacon
- Salt

Preparation:

Toast the sliced up bacon in some oil, put in the onion slices, then add the finely sliced peppers, add some salt and boil it under a lid.

Once the peppers are soft, add the finely sliced tomatoes and boil some more. Serve it with fresh bread.

16. Stuffed chicken thigh

Ingredients:

- 4 chicken thighs
- 6 rolls
- 4 cooked eggs
- 1 raw egg

- 250 g chicken liver
- 1 onion
- Some fat
- Salt
- Black pepper
- Marjoram
- Parsley
- Seasoning

Preparation:

Wash and skin the chicken thighs, then add some salt. Prepare the stuffing. Soak the rolls and squeeze out the water.

Slice up the onion, toast it on some oil and fry it with the washed chicken liver.

Boil the eggs then crack them open and slice them into cubes.

Finely slice up the parsley. Mix the rolls, the liver, the eggs with one raw egg and the parsley.

Season it with salt, black pepper and marjoram. Bake it in an oily baking oven.

17. Plum dumpling

Ingredients:

- 1000 g of potatoes
- 300 g of flour
- Plum (fresh or compote)
- Cinnamon
- Sugar
- Salt
- Breadcrumbs

- Powdered sugar

Preparation:

Boil the potatoes without peeling them, once done, pour cold water onto them and start peeling, squeeze them and mix with 300 g of flour and a bit of salt. Add some flour to a board and use a rolling pin on the dough.

Roll it into 7x7 cm long, half a finger thick squares.

Put one seedless plum into the centers of these, and put cinnamon sugar into the seed's place.

Mold it into a ball with our hands. Boil 3 liters of water with some salt, and boil these dumplings.

While they're boiling, boil a cube of margarine and add some breadcrumbs.

Once the dumplings are at the top of the water, leave them for four more minutes, then filter it and put them into the breadcrumbs. Add powdered sugar when serving.

18. Kebab skewer

Ingredients:

- 4 slices of boneless pork chop
- 250 g of pork liver
- 8 mushrooms
- 4 potatoes
- 4 slices of British bacon

- 1 big onion
- Salt
- Black pepper
- 4 sticks
- 4 slices of bread

Preparation:

Tenderize the 4 slices of boneless pork chops into thin slices, add some salt and black pepper.

Grab the 250 g of pork liver and cut it into four slices, add salt and black pepper. Cut the British bacon into four pieces as well.

Clean the onion and slice it up into circles, wash the mushrooms and cut the potatoes into 16 circles.

When skewering, the bacon should be next to the liver, and there should be salted potato circles everywhere.

The onion circle should be in the middle, and mushrooms should be at the end of the stick.

Heat the oven, and put a baking pan under the skewers with bread so that the tasty oil gets on the bread. Bake it for about 20 minutes.

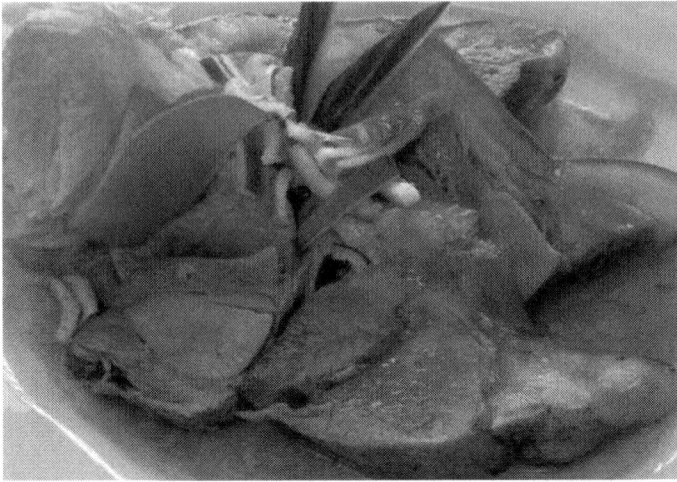

19. Boiled hand of pork

Ingredients:

- 1 big hand of pork
- 30 grams of garlic
- 10 grams of red pepper
- 2 bay leaves
- 4 whole black pepper
- 60 grams of onion
- 20 grams of salt

- 50 grams of red onion

Preparation:

Clean the hand of pork and boil it. Add spices and the half of the onion and garlic. Boil until soft.

Once the meat has separated from the bones, take it out and paste it with the rest of the pressed garlic, and some red pepper.

Cool it in the fridge. Slice it into thin slices and put it back into the bone. Serve it with thin slices of garlic, green pepper and tomato.

20. Bean salad

Ingredients:

- 50 g of white beans
- 1 onion
- 2 cloves of garlic
- 1 tablespoon of pumpkin seed oil
- 1 dl of wine vinegar
- 1 bay leaf
- 1 teaspoon of sugar
- a pinch of ground black pepper
- Salt

Preparation:

Soak the beans in water the night before, then add some salt and bay leaves, boil until soft, then cool it.

Prepare the salad dressing with pumpkin seed oil, wine vinegar, salt, sugar, finely sliced onion, garlic, black pepper and water, and pour it onto the beans.

21. Goose liver served in its fat

Ingredients:

- 50 g of goose liver
- 50 g of goose fat
- 0.5 liter of oil
- The juice of a half lemon
- Ground black pepper
- 1 onion
- 2 bouillon cubes

- Salt
- Red pepper
- 1 rosemary
- 0.5 liter of milk

Preparation:

Wash the rosemary in cold milk with lemon, soak the goose liver for two hours then let it dry.

Put the goose fat in a bowl, add some water and boil it.

Then we begin melting the fat, add two bouillon cubes.

Then put in the liver.

Cover the bowl and boil it for 20 minutes, then boil it without the lid. Turn it occasionally, and once done, put it on a plate.

Put red pepper on the fat and pour it onto the liver. Let it cool, then slice it and serve with brown bread.

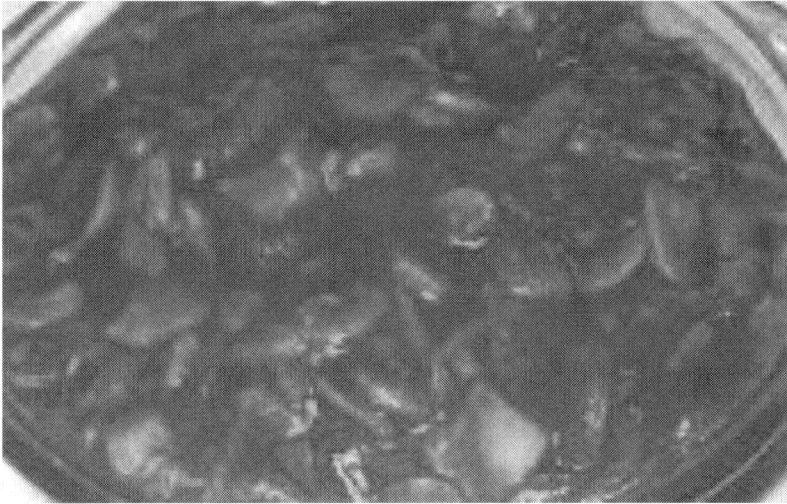

22. Swedish mushroom salad

Ingredients:

- For 8 person:
- 600 grams champignon mushroom
- 1 onion
- 150 grams of tomato puree
- 1 dl of oil

- 2 bay leaves
- 1 lemon
- 1 ladle of dried thyme
- Salt
- Black pepper
- Some powdered sugar
- Sweetener

Preparation:

Toast the finely sliced onion on the oil, then add the washed and finely cut mushrooms.

Toast them together for a few minutes then add the tomato puree. Add the lemon juice, bay leaves, thyme and some ground black pepper. Add some sugar or salt. Take out the bay leaves and put it in a glass bowl, decorate it with a lemon and parsley. It's a great side dish for cold meats.

23. Lentils salad with gamey meat

Ingredients:

- 200 g of lentils
- 80 g of mushrooms
- 1 dl of oil
- 100 g of onion
- 80 g of cucumber with vinegar
- 200 g cooked game meat
- 1 lemon
- Mustard

- 0.5 liters of red wine
- Capers
- Black pepper
- A quarter of cabbage
- Salt

Preparation:

Wash the lentils in salted water. Toast the mushrooms on oil with onions, then slice up the cucumber and the game meat.

Prepare a dressing from the rest of the oil, lemon, mustard, black pepper, capers. Put them in a bowl, add some grated horseradish and a bit of cabbage.

Pour the salad into it and put it in the fridge for 3 hours.

Enjoy your meal!

24. Aspic chicken stew

Ingredients:

- 2000 g if chicken
- 50 g of fat
- 100 g of onion
- Salt
- Red pepper
- 150 g of gelatin

Preparation:

Wash the chicken, slice it up and wash it again.

Slice up the onion, toast it on the fat, add the red pepper, then the chicken, add some salt and black pepper and boil it under a lid until soft.

Take out the meat and the bone. Put it on a bowl, decorate it with green pepper and tomato, cool it down.

Soak the gelatin, then put it into the bowl of water where the chicken was boiled, add 3 dl of more water, add some spices and boil it slowly. Filter and cool it down, then boil it onto the cool chicken.

25. Crab salad a la Zala

Ingredients:

- 1000 g of crab meat a la Zala
- 300 grams of mayonnaise
- 200 grams of whipped cream
- 5 boiled eggs
- 1 lemon
- 1 cabbage
- Half a bouquet of parsley leaves
- Half a bouquet of fresh dill
- Nutmeg powdered sugar
- Mustard
- Ketchup
- Cognac

Preparation:

Put the mayonnaise in a bowl with powdered sugar, mustard, lemon, finely cut dill and parsley.

Mix it well. Add the crab meat and the boiled eggs that are cut into cubes.

Mix it with salt, cognac, ketchup and nutmeg, then put it in the fridge. Serve it in precooled glass bowls.

Decorate it with boiled eggs, cabbage, fresh dill, then add the sauce.

Crab sauce:

Mix the mayonnaise with cognac, whipped cream and crab oil.

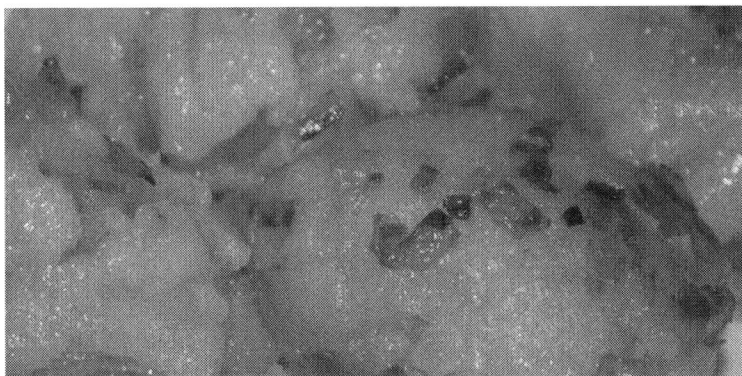

26. Potato ganca

Ingredients:

- 1000 g of potatoes

- Flour
- Salt
- Fat
- Breadcrumbs

Preparation:

Clean the potatoes, cut and boil them. Empty the water from the bowl, but a bit should remain. Break the potatoes and mix it with salt and some flour.

Boil this and keep stirring. Get it out with a spoon to a plate. Once done, twist the dough into toasted breadcrumbs. Serve with sugar.

If we prefer salt, you can toast some onions or bacon, cottage cheese or sour cream.

27. Shepherd meat

Ingredients:

- 600 g beef
- 250 g egg barley
- 400 g potatoes
- 80 g onion
- 50 g fat
- 1dkg red pepper
- 2 cloves of garlic
- 60 g ratatouille
- Salt
- Cumin seed

Preparation:

Toast the finely cut onion in fat. Once done, add some red peppers, pour some water into it, add the pressed garlic, cumin seeds and the meat cut into cubes.

If the meat starts to soften, add the ratatouille.

Meanwhile, toast the egg barley and cut the potato into cubes and add it to the meat, pour 0.6 liters of boiling water into it and keep boiling it under a lid.

Decorate it with pepper and tomatoes. Shepherds used to cook this in a cauldron for dinner.

28. Cholent with smoked pork loin

Ingredients:

- 700 g raw smoked pork loin
- 400 g big beans
- 1 onion
- 100 g pearl barley
- 100 g fat
- 4 eggs
- 1 teaspoon of red pepper
- 1 cloves of garlic
- Ground black pepper

Preparation:

Prepare the cholent in a water soaked pot. Filter the pre soaked beans and pearl barley, add some finely cut and washed onion, pressed garlic and pour these into the pot.

Make a small nest out of the beans and put the meat into it. The meat should be soaked in cold water the day before.

Put washed, raw eggs around it with their shells.

Add some red pepper and black pepper, and some fat and enough water so that it is submerged.

Cover the pot, put it in a cold oven and heat it for 15 minutes on lower temperatures, and then for 20 minutes in higher temperatures, and for 3 hours in moderately high temperature.

Once done, take it out of the oven, stir it with a fork and slice up the smoked meat. Remove the shells of the eggs and cut them in half.

Put the eggs and the bacon slices on top of the beans when serving.

29. With kidney marrow

Ingredients:

- 50 g pork kidney
- 1 piece of pig brain
- 1 onion
- 1 tablespoon of fat
- 1 tablespoon of tarragon vinegar
- Salt
- Black pepper
- Marjoram
- Half a coffee spoon of hot mustard

Preparation:

Wash the kidneys, take off the membrane and finely cut them.

Put the brain into a hot water seasoned with a spoon of tarragon vinegar, and once boiled, take it out and clean it, then finely slice it up.

Toast it on some fat, add the finely sliced onion and toast the kidneys. Once done, add the brain with a bit of marjoram and mustard, then add some salt, black pepper and boil it for a bit.

30. Pike with beans

Ingredients:

- 350 grams of beans
- 900 grams pike fillet
- 50 grams of celery
- 50 grams onion
- 100 ml cream
- 20 grams of salt

- 50 grams of butter
- 60 grams grated cheese

Preparation:

Wash the beans, boil it in salted water until soft, then add the finely cut celery. The prepared pike fillet should be put into a buttery bowl, pour the baked beans into it.

Add some sliced onion and some of the bean's water, and boil it under a lid.

Add the cream with grated cheese, put it in the oven until the cheese starts to melt. Serve it with rice.

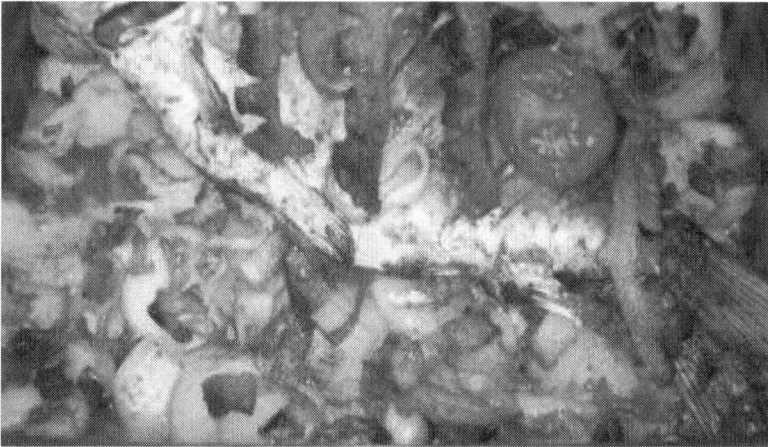

31. Serbian carp

Ingredients:

- 800 grams of carp
- 100 grams smoked bacon
- 1 kg potatoes
- 2 onion
- 4 pieces of green pepper
- 4 tomatoes

- 4 tablespoon of oil
- 1 tablespoon of red pepper
- 1 coffee spoon of cherry pepper
- 2 dl sour cream
- 1 tablespoon of flour
- Salt

Preparation:

Cut the carp into four equal pieces. Put them onto a board with their skin on the top and make many incisions.

Put one thin slice of bacon into the cuts. Then add some salt. Boil the potatoes in cold water without peeling them, then peel them and cut them into circles. Wash the onion, take out the pepper's seeds and the stalk of the tomatoes. Put the onion into some oil. Slice up the pepper and the tomatoes and pour it into the onion, toast it for 5 minutes, then add some salt and red pepper, then some cherry pepper cream, add some flour with cream, boil it for 3 minutes. Put the potatoes into a bigger baking oven, pour the ratatouille with cream onto it, and put the carp around it. Bake it for 15 minutes.

32. Székely catfish ragout

Ingredients:

- 900 grams catfish fillet
- 25 grams sour cabbage
- 80 grams onion
- 10 grams red pepper
- 100 grams green pepper

- 20 grams salt
- 2 dl cream
- 60 grams flour
- 5 grams garlic
- 100 grams tomatoes

Preparation:

Slice the onion into small pieces and toast them on some fat, add some pepper and some water.

Add a washed cabbage and a pepper cut into cubes, and some tomatoes, and then boil it slowly.

Make a mix out of sour cream and flour then pour it onto the cabbage.

Cut the catfish fillet into cubes, add it to the cabbage and boil it for 20 minutes. Serve it with pepper and sour cream.

33. Shepherd boy's roast

Ingredients:

- 600 grams pork loin
- 80 grams smoked bacon
- 80 grams smoked sausage
- 60 grams green peas
- 80 grams fat
- 100 grams onion
- 60 grams ratatouille
- Spice pepper
- Salt

Preparation:

Melt the smoked bacon cut into cubes, toast it in its fat, add some finely cut onions, then some spice pepper, add some salt and pour in the ratatouille, green peas and the sliced sausage, then boil them together.

Toast the sliced meats with some salt on fat. Put them on a plate and pour it down with the ragout. I recommend toast potatoes as a side dish.

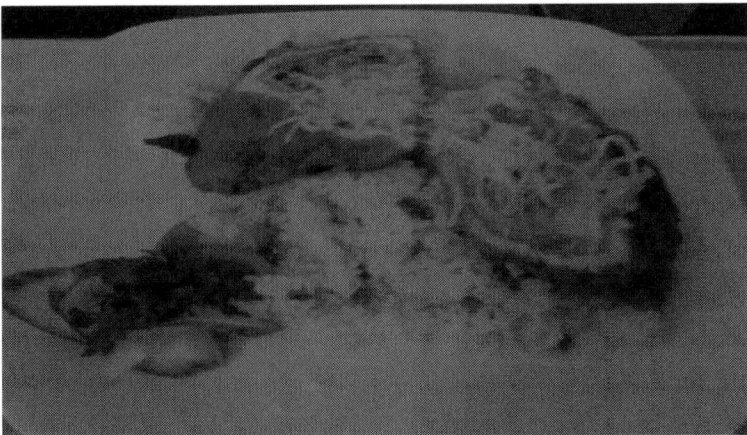

34. Fried calf leg

Ingredients:

- 2 pieces of calf leg
- 1 onion
- 1 carrot
- 1 parsley roots
- 1 celery roots
- Salt

For the breadcrumbs:

- 2 eggs
- 150 g breadcrumbs
- 100 g flour
- Oil for cooking

Preparation:

Wash the calf legs and boil it until soft in water with some salt, and add the vegetables cut into cubes and a whole onion.

Cool it down, take out the bones, add some salt and put them in breadcrumbs. Cook it well in a bowl with some oil.

35. Roast a la Csáki

Ingredients:

- 1000 g roast meat

- 120 g fat
- 200 g onion
- 350 g green pepper
- 200 g tomatoes
- 5 eggs
- 120 g smoked bacon
- 4 dl sour cream
- 50 g flour
- 10 g red pepper
- 20 g black pepper and salt

Preparation:

Cut the roast meat into evenly sliced pieces; add some salt and black pepper. Toast some finely cut bacon and add some finely cut onion, green pepper and tomatoes then add some salt and boil it.

Once it is soft, add the mixed eggs and boil until it gets dense.

Put the roast slices on a plate and add the stuffing, put it on a skewer and tie it with a thin rope.

Add salt, twist them in flour and cook it in its fat, once both sides are done, put it in a plate and keep it warm.

Toast some finely cut onion in fat, and then add some red pepper and water. Add salt and pour it onto the roast.

Boil it for a while in medium temperature. If the meat is half-soft, cut some tomatoes and add some pepper.

Once the meat is soft and tender, take it out, take off the ropes.

The remaining juices should be mixed with sour cream, flour. Serve it with noodles.

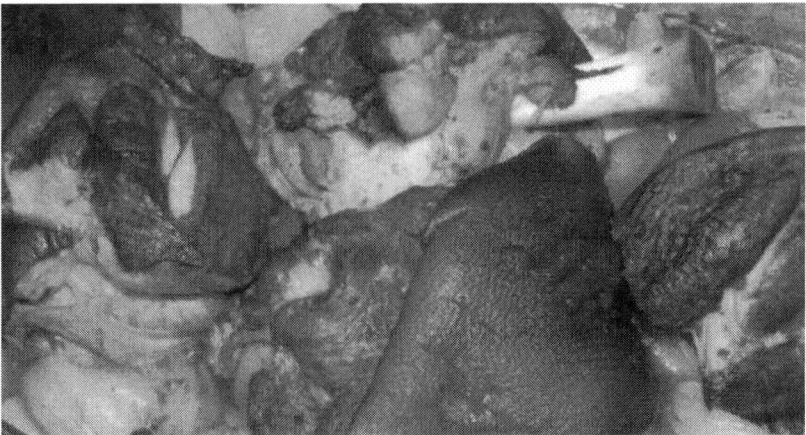

36. Pork leg a la Pékné

Ingredients:

- 2 big rear hand of pork
- 2 smaller front hand of pork
- 1 tablespoon of salt
- 1 small soon of black pepper
- 1 onion
- 2 bay leaves
- 4 cloves of garlic

Side dish:

Ingredients:

- 2000 g potatoes
- 300 g onion
- Salt

- Ground black pepper
- Red pepper
- Marjoram
- 1 parsley
- 4 teaspoons of oil

Preparation:

Wash the hand of pork, put it in a bowl and pour water into it so that it is submerged.

Add some black pepper, onion, bay leaves, garlic. Boil it for 2 hours until tender. Once done, take it out and put it in a big oven pan.

Cut some potatoes and onions for side dish. Add some salt, black pepper, red pepper, marjoram and parsley, mix them well with oil.

Put these around the hand of pork, and bake it for one hour at 180 degrees Celsius.

When serving it, take off the meat from the bones and cut them into cubes. Serve it with potatoes and pickles.

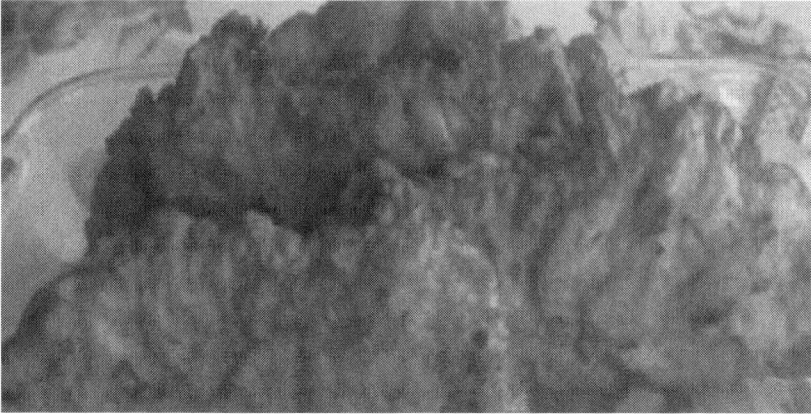

37. Roast a la Göcsej

Ingredients:

- 600 grams of pork loin
- 100 grams of smoked sausage
- 80 grams of smoked bacon
- 10 grams of garlic
- 80 grams onion
- 80 grams flour

- Salt
- Black pepper
- Red pepper

Preparation:

Cut double slices from the loin, add salt, black pepper, pressed garlic and onion. Add some sliced smoked sausage and bacon, and then stitch the openings of the meat.

Twist it in flour with paprika, and then cook it.

38. Butcher's stew

Ingredients:

- 800 g pork scapula
- 150 g bacon
- 50 g fat
- 150 g onion
- 30 g tomato puree
- 1 cloves of garlic
- Salt
- 3 pieces of vinegar cucumber
- Black pepper
- 1 dl white wine

Preparation:

Cut the meat into long strips and wash it. Cut the bacon then toast it with some onion.

Once done, add the tomato puree and the finely cut garlic. Mix it well, add the white wine and cook it for two minutes.

Then add it to the meat, add some salt and black pepper to the meat and boil them. Once tender, add the sliced vinegar cucumbers and boil it for five more minutes.

39. Rooster testicle stew

Ingredients:

- 500 g rooster testicle
- 300 g rooster comb
- 1 onion

- 2 purple onion
- 4 cloves of garlic
- 3 teaspoons of oil
- Salt
- Black pepper
- Red pepper
- Half a teaspoon of ginger powder
- 1 dl dry red wine

Preparation:

Toast the finely cut onion and garlic on the oil and add some red pepper.

Add the washed rooster comb and the rooster testicles, toast them together.

Add some wine and 1 dl of water, add salt and ginger powder.

Boil it until tender and thick.

Cut the purple onion into circles, add salt and decorate the meal with them.

BOOK 2
Hungarian soups

Foreword

I would like to highlight that this book is about cooking at home. This is not about restaurant wonders where the customers are enchanted with beautiful-looking dishes.

This book has no wonders or over the top decorations, waiters and so on. This book is about our own kitchen and regular kitchen ingredients. This book is about our own two hands, hearts and everyday cooking.

Recognition will come from our family, relatives, friends and guests, but more importantly, we must be able to create something that is good.

What is this recognition, you may ask? Simple; 'Thank you! It was delicious!' and so on. However, the best recognition is when all the food is gone. My goal with this and my previous book / "Hungarian cuisine – Main dishes" / is to give you my recipes so that you can get this kind of recognition as well.

Book description

Gastronomy is a part of culture, which shows us the development of centuries. There are many ingredients that play an important role in the Hungarian cuisine, but we easily forget about these in our everyday lives.

A meal can reveal things about our ancestors, as these recipes went from parents to children.

The Hungarian goulash is the most important meal in the Great Hungarian Plain. Cooking competitions are organized in order to keep the image of the Hungarian goulash.

The same can be said about our other meals such as Hungarian Fisherman's soup, sausages, sheep goulash, etc.

Hungary has a great history of animal husbandry and agriculture. Hungarian cuisine is full of rich flavors and spices.

Soups are one of the most important part of Hungarian cuisine. Soups are usually served with meat, pasta or vegetables.

The most important ingredient in all of them is the famous Hungarian paprika.

Not many know the great taste of traditional Hungarian cooking as our cuisine is not as widespread as others.

This is another reason why you should check out these Hungarian soup recipes so that you can surprise your family and guests with flavors they never tasted before!

This cookbook details great tasting meals that are easily made for beginner and advanced cooks alike.

Meet the mysteries of the Hungarian cuisine and learn the technique to making delicious, Hungarian meals!

What do you get?

I will share with you the recipes of this country of 10 million. Every meal is a special delicacy.

What is even more special about this book is that every meal is a soup, most of these contain meat.

Our most famous soups are the goulash, Fisherman's soup, bean goulash and the golden broth, which we prepare for celebration.

I will show you one method of making these meals. This book teaches you how to make meals that you can serve to your family, relatives and friends. I will show you how to prepare and cook these meals step by step.

This is not about calories! I'm sure that you can find yourself in this book, besides the filling, delicious meals that contain little calories.

I want the buyers of my books to say that this is an excellent cookbook! I'd like my readers to be satisfied. I had my fair share of failures, but we must never give up. As the saying goes – practice makes perfect.

This not only applies to gastronomy, but to everything in our lives. If you think you're comfortable in the kitchen, trust me, I can surprise you!

Vegetables:
Kohlrabi

Cabbage, Pepper

Garlic, Onion

Turni, Carrot

1. Potato soup with bacon

It's important to have a flavorful and filling soup – so I will show you this soup recipe full of calories, bacon and potatoes. It doesn't take a lot of time and you can make it in a bowl, it's also great as a main course.

Ingredients:

- 3 stripes of bacon cubes
- 1 sliced onion
- 2 peeled and sliced carrot
- 2 peeled and sliced white carrot
- 3 tablespoon flour
- 100 g boiled ham
- 500 g sliced potatoes
- Sage
- Black pepper
- Bay leaves
- Salt
- 6 tablespoon sour cream

Preparation:

Fry the bacon and the ham in some oil. Add the onion and toast them together.

Then add the sliced vegetables, and once half done, add the potatoes as well.

Add some water and spices, and once the vegetables are done, make some thickening with flour and sour cream.

Add it while stirring and the soup is done!

2. Cheese cream soup in bread

Great for lunch and dinner. Easy to made and delicious. Light and healthy, great for the whole family.

Ingredients:

- 4 bread
- 1 onion
- 2 cloves of garlic
- Some oil
- 250 g trappista cheese
- 2 dl cooking cream
- 1,5 l broth
- Red pepper
- Salt
- Ground white pepper
- Ground nutmeg

Preparation:

Cut the top of the bread, take out the insides but leave a bit. Peel the onions and slice them into cubes.

Toast the onion on some oil then add the pressed garlic. Take it off from the fire, add the red pepper and the insides of the bread, then mix them together and put it onto the fire, toast the bread a bit.

Add 0.5 l of soup, and then boil for 15 minutes. Stir it so it doesn't burn!

Once done, make a puree from it with a hand-held blender.

Add the rest of the broth, and then grate some cheese. Keep stirring it while the cheese melts.

Once the cheese has melted, add the cooking cream, mix it together, add some spice and boil it for another 10-12 minutes.

Wait for it to cool, and then serve it in a bread. Decorate it with parsley, but you can serve it with grated cheese, toasted bacon or toasted bread cubes.

3. Meatball soup

Great for lunch or dinner, even for a main course. You can add some hot peppers so that it becomes a real, fiery Hungarian meal!

Ingredients:

- 1 onion

- 3 cloves of garlic
- 1,5 l broth
- 2 tablespoon oil
- 50 g semolina
- 250 g minced meat
- 2 eggs
- Red pepper
- Thyme
- Salt
- Black pepper

Preparation:

Toast the sliced onion and garlic on some oil. Take it off the fire, then add some minced meat, semolina, 2 eggs and some spices, then mix it. Let it rest for 10 minutes, then make some balls from the mix and boil it in a soup.

The balls should be evenly sized. You can also add vegetables and even black pepper.

4. Bean goulash

Bean goulash is one of the most popular homemade meals, it's very filling.

Hungarian families often prepare this on the weekends, sometimes they do it outside in a big cauldron (bogrács) with friends.

Ingredients:

- 500 g bean
- 500 g pork thigh or beef leg sliced into cubes
- 1 big onion
- Fat
- Red pepper
- Carrot
- White carrot
- 1/2 celery
- Celery greens
- Salt
- Black pepper

Preparation:

Cut the onion into cubes, toast it on some fat, add the meat and toast them together with some salt and black pepper.

Add some red pepper to the meat, then pour some water into the bowl. Boil it until the meat is soft and tender.

Then add the beans that were soaked for a night, then add the sliced vegetables as well. Add some celery greens, then some water and add spices,

you can also add hot pepper. It's served with a lot of sour cream.

5. Tomato soup

It's a delicious and light soup for lunch or dinner with letter shaped pasta. It's children's favorite, maybe because of the pasta.

Ingredients:

- 1 onion
- 1 liter tomato juice
- Some oil
- 1 tablespoon flour
- Some sugar
- Some Salt
- Letter shaped pasta
- Celery stem or 1/2 head of celery

Preparation:

Prepare some frying ingredients from oil and flour. Add the cold tomato juice and mix it together. Add the onion, celery or celery stem, then some sugar, salt and black pepper.

Don't cut the celery or the onion. Boil it, and once it starts to boil, boil for another 10-15 minutes. Boil the letter shaped pasta in water with salt, and put

it into the soup when serving it. It's a delicious meal, children's favorite.

6. Pumpkin cream soup

This is a delicious, light soup, which is great for the first course of lunch or dinner. You can prepare it in a few minutes and it's a very light meal. Children also tend to like this as well.

Ingredients:

- 1500 g pumpkin
- 1 onion
- 2 cloves of garlic
- 1 tablespoon olive oil
- 1 l water
- 1 broth cubes
- 2 dl cream
- Salt
- Black pepper

Preparation:

Peel the pumpkin, take out the seeds and cut it into cubes.

Put 2 tablespoons of olive oil into the pan, then add the onion slices and toast it, then add the pressed garlic as well. Stir it so that they don't burn.

Take off the pan from the fire. Add a broth soup cube into water and boil for about 3 minutes.

Add the toast onion and the pumpkin cubes and boil for another 10-15 minutes.

Add some salt and black pepper. You can use a hand-held blender to make it creamier.

Put it back to the fire, add some sour cream and

boil for 2-3 minutes. Serve it with toast bread cubes or bacon.

7. Garlic cream soup

I love soups and I eat them every day. One of my favorites is the garlic cream soup because it's healthy and very delicious.

A garlic a day keeps the cold and other illnesses away. You can prepare this meal in a few minutes. Take care of your health!

Ingredients:

- 1 onion
- 1 tablespoon fat
- 2,5 liter water
- 10 cloves of garlic
- 2 potatoes
- 3,5 dl cream
- 1500 g tablespoon flour
- 3 tablespoon sour cream 20%
- Salt
- Black pepper or other condiment

Preparation:

Slice the onion and the potatoes into small cubes, toast the onion on some fat, then add the potatoes and garlic.

Add some salt, black pepper or some other store-bought condiment.

Add some water, boil it until it's soft and mix it with a blender.

Add some sour cream and flour, mix it well, add the cream and boil it. Serve it with toast bread cubes and grated cheese.

8. Fisherman's soup a la Baja

Many people like the Hungarian Fisherman's soup. Most Christmas meals in the evening open with this soup in Hungary.

There are many variations that come from different parts of Hungary such as the Balaton, Baja or Szeged.

They didn't pasteurize the soup around the Tisza. Catfish, sturgeon, starlet, carp were often used for the Fisherman's soup in Szeged.

Fisherman's soup in Baja was made from only carp, and it's served with a home-made thick soup pasta called gyufa pasta.

They also use mostly carp around the Balaton. They make the soup from small fish and also use the head and the tail of the carp. Fisherman's soup is delicious and healthy, and almost necessary after a good cottage cheese pasta.

Ingredients:

- 2500 – 3000 g carp
- 3 big onion
- 3 tablespoon ground sweet red pepper
- Salt
- 4-5 pieces of hot pepper
- 1000 g soup pasta

Preparation:

Peel off the scales of the fish and take out the roes, don't add salt!

Slice the fish and add some salt. Only add the head if you've already taken out its fangs, otherwise the soup will be bitter.

Let it rest for an hour. Peel the onion and cut it into small cubes.

Once one hour has passed, put the fish into the bowl and add the onion, then add 0.33 liters of water per kilogram of fish.

Boil it, and once it starts to foam, add some red pepper, then 15 minutes later the insides and the hot pepper.

Taste it, add some spices if you need. Boil it for another 10-15 minutes, and don't forget to boil the pasta.

According to traditions, we serve the pasta then add the soup into the plate.

9. Broth

Ingredients:

- Turkey neck, chicken thigh, chicken breast, beef brisket, pork chop, bones
- 1 medium onion
- 4-5 cloves of garlic
- 4 carrot
- 1 medium celery cut in half
- 2-3 celery leaves
- Some parsley
- 1 green pepper
- 1 teaspoon of black pepper
- Salt
- Some ground cumin
- Spices according to your taste
- Some kale
- Half kohlrabi

Preparation:

Wash the meats in a big bowl and add some cold water until half of the bowl is covered. Boil it and filter the foam. While it's boiling, prepare the vegetables.

Peel the carrot, garlic, green pepper and put it into the bowl, then add the kale cut in half, but the hard part should be cut into four pieces.

Peel the onion, but leave some of the shell on it so that the soup will be gold colored, then add some celery leaves and parsley, and tie them together so that you'll have an easier job when filtering it.

Put the vegetables in, then add some water until so that there will be around 3-5 cm of space remaining.

Add some salt, black pepper, ground cumin and keep boiling it.

You don't have to boil it, but keep checking the meat – we use a variety of meat, and if one is tender but the others are not, take out the soft ones.

While it's boiling, boil some water for the pasta. Once done, let it rest for a while, then take out the vegetables and the meats, then filter the soup. If you like boiled garlic, onion, green pepper, and then you can also eat it.

Serve it with the soup pasta and add some hot pepper if you'd like, and serve the boiled meats with vinegar and horseradish. Enjoy your meal!

10. Semolina noodle soup

This is a simple, light, delicious soup, which is great for the first course as lunch or dinner.

You can prepare this in a matter of a few minutes. It's great for vegetarians as this has no meat.

Ingredients:

- 3 big carrot
- 2 vegetables
- 1 vegetable green
- 1 celery green
- 1 onion
- 2 cloves of garlic
- 3 tablespoon of oil
- 2 broth cubes
- 1 egg
- 50-70 g semolina
- Ground black pepper
- Salt

Preparation:

Toast the vegetables cut into cubes on some fat, then add the onion and garlic.

Add about 1.5 liters of water, then the broth cubes, spice with salt and black pepper and boil for 15-20 minutes.

While boiling, stir an egg with a fork, add some salt and black pepper, then some finely cut vegetables. Add some semolina so that it's thick like sour cream.

Leave it for about 7 minutes, then make some pasta with it and put it in the soup.

Boil it for another 15 minutes until the pasta is done, then serve it. Decorate it with celery greens.

11. Fruit soup

A delicious fruit soup for lunch or dinner, you can make it with a variety of different fruit.

Ingredients:

- 1000 g mixed fruit
- Apple
- Plum
- Pear
- Peach cubes
- A bit of lemon
- 3 tablespoons of flour
- Some cinnamon
- 6 clove
- Sugar

Preparation:

Slice up the fruit into cubes and boil it in water. Add some cinnamon, clove, sugar and some lemon.

Then mix 0.5 liters of milk in a different bowl with 3 spoons of flour. Mix and boil for one minute. You can serve it cold or hot. Enjoy your meal!

12. Frankfurter soup

A great, filling meal for lunch or dinner.

Ingredients:

- 1000 g frankfurter
- 1000 g kale

- 3 cloves of garlic
- 40 g marjoram
- Salt
- Black pepper
- Ground paprika
- 1 container of sour cream
- Some oil
- 3 spoons of flour

Preparation:

Slice up the kale into stripes and boil it. Add some salt, black pepper and marjoram. Then slice up the frankfurter and fry it on some oil, then add them into the soup.

Then fry some flour on oil, then add ground pepper, sour cream and mix it with the soup. This gives it a nice, sour taste.

13. Palóc soup

Palóc soup is similar to the Hungarian goulash, but it's lighter and has a bit of a sour taste.

You can use beef, pork or lamb.

Ingredients:

- 800 g beef
- 2 tablespoon oil
- 1 onion
- 300 g potato
- 500 g green bean
- 1 tablespoon flour
- 1 container of sour cream
- 1 small spoon of Red pepper
- Salt
- 2 bay leaves

Preparation:

Fry the sliced up onion, then add some red pepper and the meat sliced up into cubes, boil it in 2 liters of water.

Add the spices and slowly boil it. Add the sliced up potato and green bean.

Then fry some flour, and pour it into the soup with sour cream.

14. Korhely soup

Sour cabbage soup with sausage or trotters. A delicacy for the New Year.

This is good for the stomach on the day after the New Year.

Ingredients:

- 1 smoked trotters or 300 g smoked sausage
- 500 g sour cabbage

- 2 tablespoon oil
- 1 tablespoon flour
- Salt
- 1 small spoon Red pepper
- Big black pepper
- Sour cream

Preparation:

Use oil and flour for frying. Add the cabbage and boil it with 1 liter of water.

Then add the sliced up trotters or sausage. Boil it well, then pour in the sour cream before serving.

15. Chicken soup a la Újház

One of the delicacies of the Hungarian cuisine.

Ingredients:

- 1 full chicken
- 300 g green peas
- 200 g mushroom
- 300 g vegetables
- 200 g carrot

Preparation:

Wash the chicken and boil it in 5 liters of cold water. Add one spoon of salt.

Once boiling, take off the foam and add some sliced up carrot and mushroom. Add some salt, ground black pepper.

Once done, take out the vegetables. Slice up the meat and make some pasta, then serve it.

16. Green bean soup

Its sour taste it great for hot summer days, but you can serve it hot as well.

Ingredients:

- 500 g green bean
- 2 liters of water
- 1 parsley
- 1 carrot
- 2 tablespoon oil
- 1 tablespoon flour
- 2 cloves of garlic
- 1 sour cream
- Salt
- A bit of red pepper

Preparation:

Clean the beans, then cut them into small, 1 cm pieces and boil it with vegetables.

Mix some oil and flour for frying and add it to the soup. You can serve it with noodles as well.

17. Fried soup

This is a great soup for stomachache or for a heavy stomach.

Ingredients:

- 2 tablespoon oil
- 1 tablespoon flour
- Salt
- 2 soup cubes
- 1 teaspoon Red pepper
- Bread cubes fried in oil

Preparation:

Mix some oil with flour and fry it with red pepper, then add 1 liter of cold water.

Add some salt, then add one broth cube and boil it for 4 minutes. Serve the bread cubes in a different plate.

18. Egg soup with cumin

Great for lunch and dinner alike.

Prepare it the same way as the fried soup, but add a teaspoon of cumin and add some water and red pepper. Once boiling, boil four whole eggs in it. Serve it with bread cubes fried in oil.

19. Dill soup

The taste of summer and spring.

Ingredients:

- 50 g butter
- 1 tablespoon of flour

- 3 eggs
- 1 raw egg yolk
- 2 dl sour cream
- Salt
- 1 pack of dill

Preparation:

Mix the butter and flour for frying, add the finely sliced dill and pour 2 liters of water into it, add some salt and boil for 6 minutes, then serve it with sour cream, egg yolk and one big egg.

20. Celery cream soup

Great, delicious soup for those looking to lose weight.

Ingredients:

- 600 g celery
- 60 g butter
- 2 liter water
- 3 dl sour cream
- 1 small spoon of sugar
- Salt
- 2 tablespoon flour

Preparation:

Wash the celery and slice it up, boil it until soft, add one broth cube, then some salt, butter and mix it with sour cream and flour. Add some sugar. Serve it with toasted bread cubes.

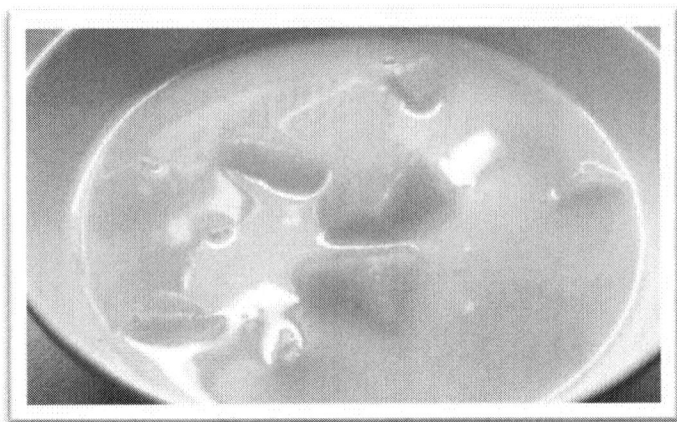

21. Quince soup

Quince is great for throat inflammation, but it's also delicious.

Ingredients:

- 600 g quince
- 160 g sugar
- 1dl cream
- 1 lemon peel
- Salt
- Ground cinnamon

Preparation:

Peel the quince, slice it up and take out the seeds. Pour 2 liters of water into it, then add the lemon peel, add some salt and sugar.

Add some cinnamon and boil it until it's soft. Then mix it with a blender.

Take out the lemon peel, add the cream and boil for 6 minutes. You can serve it cold as well.

22. Lebbencs soup

It's a simple, filling and cheap soup. You can also do it with carrot, white carrot, celery.

You can use hot pepper as well.

Ingredients:

- 250 g potatoes
- 1 onion
- 2 cloves of garlic
- 150 g smoked bacon
- 250 g lebbencs pasta
- 2,5 l water
- 1 pack of parsley
- Ground red pepper
- Black pepper
- Ground spice cumin
- 4-5 bay leaves

- Salt

Preparation:

Slice up the bacon into cubes, cook it.

Take out the bacon, then toast the onion in the bacon's fat.

Then add the lebbencs pasta and toast it with the onion.

Add some red pepper, ground spice cumin, black pepper, salt, some bay leaves and some pressed garlic, mic it well and add a liter of water.

Let it soak for a few minutes.

Add the potato sliced into cubes, pour enough water so that the potatoes are submerged. Boil it and add some spices if you must.

Once the potato and the pasta are tender, serve it with parsley and bacon cubes.

23. Cauliflower soup

A light soup without meat, but you can add sausages, pasta or potato.

Ingredients:

- 1 big cauliflower

- 2 white carrots
- 3 carrots
- 1 onion
- 3 cloves of pressed garlic
- 1 pack of parsley
- Red pepper
- 2.5 dl sour cream
- 4 tablespoon of fine flour
- 2 tablespoon sunflower oil
- Black pepper
- Salt
- 2 l water

Preparation:

Take apart the cauliflower, wash it well. Peel and slice the carrots.

Slice up the onion and press the garlic.

Heat up some oil, add the onion, toast it then add the garlic and toast them together for 2 minutes.

Add some spice pepper, stir it, add the carrot, then pour enough water to cover it.

Add some salt, black pepper, boil for 15 minutes, then add the cauliflower and pour some water onto it.

Boil for 25-30 minutes until the cauliflower is tender.

Then mix some sour cream with flour, add three tablespoons of it into the soup. Boil for 5-7 minutes, then add the parsley, boil for 1 more minutes and the cauliflower soup is done.

Enjoy your meal!

24. Outlaw soup a la Bakony

A quick, simple, but filling soup made from two different kinds of meat.

Ingredients:

- 400 g beef brisket
- 2 pairs of chicken thighs
- 300 g vegetable mix
- 2 onion
- 1 egg

- Flour
- Hot paprika
- Whole black pepper
- Salt

Preparation:

Slice up the beef, boil it in cold water. Add some salt and whole black pepper.

Let it boil, and once almost tender, add the chicken thighs and the vegetables, then add some onion and hot pepper.

Make some pasta from flour and an egg, put it in the soup and boil for two more minutes. Serve it with fresh, soft bread. Enjoy your meal!

25. Beetroot soup

Beetroot is a red vitamin bomb! It's low in carbohydrates and calories.

There are tons of vitamins in it.

It's high in iron, which helps your immune system and beetroot is a great ingredient for lots of meals!

Ingredients:

- 600 g beetroot, sugar
- 1 lemon
- 1 tablespoon of butter
- 1 egg yolk
- 2,5 dl sour cream
- Fresh dill
- Black pepper
- Salt

Preparation:

Wash the beetroot, peel it and slice it up.

Add some sugar and salt to a bowl of water and boil the beetroot in it, then filter it out and take it in the soup.

Add some salt, black pepper and dill, then some lemon juice.

Boil it, put in the butter, the sour cream and the egg yolk. Mix it well. Boil it while stirring, make it thicker, and add spices if you need it.

26. Plum soup

Ingredients:

- 1000 g plum
- 1 lemon
- 3 tablespoon flour
- Some cinnamon
- 4 cloves
- Sugar

Preparation:

Pour water into a bowl, then add some cinnamon, cloves, sugar and one slice of lemon, then boil it.

Take out the seeds from the plums and put it in the water, then mix together half a liter of milk with three spoons of flour.

Mix it with the soup. You can serve it hot or cold.

27. Meatball soup with snail dough

Ingredients:

- 300 g minced meat (e.g. pork shoulder)
- 3 carrots
- 2 parsley roots
- 1 slice of celery
- 1 onion
- 3 cloves of garlic
- 1 tablespoon of flavoring
- 200 g snail dough
- 1 tablespoon of flour
- 1 egg
- 2 tablespoon of oil
- 1,5 l water
- Salt
- Ground black pepper

Preparation:

Add some salt and black pepper to the minced meat.

Add the egg and mix it well.

Wet your hands and make small balls from this mixture.

Clean the vegetables, the onion and the garlic and slice them up into circles.

Heat up some oil, add the sliced up onion and toast them.

Then add the small garlic slices and the vegetables, mix them together and toast for a few minutes.

Add some salt, black pepper and flour, then mix them together and add some water.

Boil it until the vegetables are semi tender, and then put in the meatloaves and the pasta.

You can make it without pasta, but it's more filling this way. You can also use hot pepper.

Serve it hot.

28. Diet celery soup

A delicious, diet soup. If you're not looking to diet, you can use toast bread cubes as well.

Ingredients:

- 4 carrots

- 3 potatoes
- 1 celery
- 7 dl water
- 2 teaspoon of basal
- 2 soup cubes
- Black pepper
- Salt

Preparation:

Wash the vegetables and peel them. Slice them up, boil it and add some spices.

Once the vegetables are tender, take them out, but them in cold water and use a blender to mix them so that they become creamy.

Pour this cream back into the soup, mix it with black pepper and basal.

29. Diet pear soup

I think everybody likes pears. This is a light, delicious fruit soup with low calories. I hope you will like it!

Ingredients:

- 7 pears
- 6 dl water

- 1.5 dl milk
- 4 teaspoons of honey
- Cinnamon
- Clove

Preparation:

Wash the pears and cut them into four pieces. Take out the ovaries and cut the fruit into cubes.

Add the honey and 1.5 dl of water. Boil it for a bit until the pears start to get tender. Boil it some more on small heat, then add the remaining water, then some milk and the spices. If the pears are tender, it's ready to be served. You can serve it cold or hot. Once slice of lemon gives it a great taste.

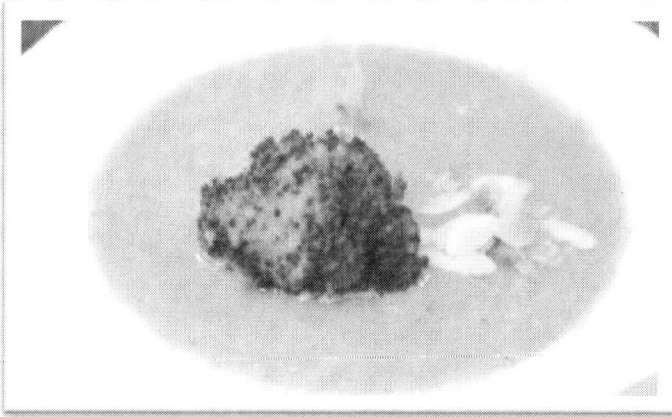

30. Broccoli cream soup with toasted almond

I wanted to make a light soup, a small fitness bomb. It's very delicious.

Ingredients:

- 350 g broccoli

- 7 dl milk
- 30 g almond
- Nutmeg
- Black pepper
- Salt

Preparation:

Wash the broccoli, let it dry for a bit then slice them up. Boil some milk.

Let it cool then boil it once more. Mix the broccoli with the milk, add some salt, black pepper and nutmeg.

Boil for 10 more minutes, and then use a blender to make it creamy.

Toast the almonds and sprinkle it on top the soup when serving it. If you like it sweet, you can add sweetener as well.

BOOK 3
Cookbook for beginners
Cold & Hot sauces

Foreword

I would like to highlight that this book is about cooking at home. This is not about restaurant wonders where the customers are enchanted with beautiful-looking dishes.

This book has no wonders or over the top decorations, waiters and so on. This book is about our own kitchen and regular kitchen ingredients. This book is about our own two hands, hearts and everyday cooking.

Recognition will come from our family, relatives, friends and guests, but more importantly, we must be able to create something that is good.

What is this recognition, you may ask? Simple; 'Thank you! It was delicious!' and so on. However, the best recognition is when all the food is gone. My goal with this and my previous books / "Hungarian cuisine - Main dishes" / /"Hungarian cuisine -Cookbook for beginners - Hungarian soups /

Is to give you my recipes so that you can get this kind of recognition as well.

Book description

Sauces provide a big variety to food in our diet. They contain essential nutrition. The color, taste, density and aroma is very important when making a sauce.

Different meals, for example, meats require different sauces. Meat from a broth is boring in itself, but it can be served as a main course with the right sauce.

When cooking fish, choose a light colored sauce with a bit of spice, but when cooking gamey meat, make a rich brown sauce. You can season it with different meat extracts. The boiling brings out tastes you wouldn't get with cold sauces.

However, cold sauces are delicious as well. For example, tartar sauce is almost essential. Hot sauces require more time, but it's not impossible to learn.

Don't be disappointed if you don't succeed at the first time. Next time, it will better! What matters is that you need to do your best, and you will be proud. You'll see how your friends, family and guests are loving the meal.

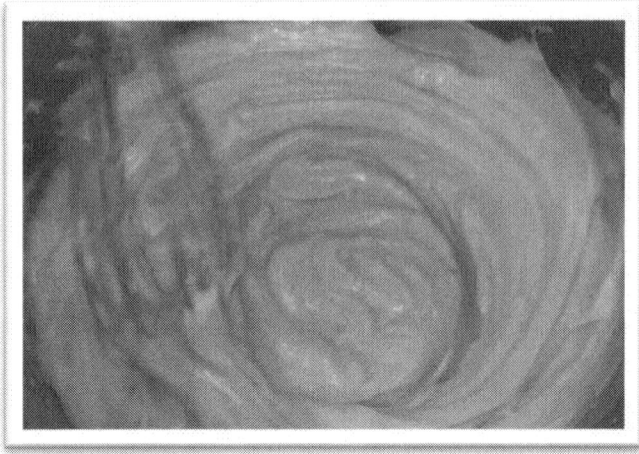

1 Mayonnaise sauce

Ingredients:

- 3 egg yolks
- 3 dl olive oil
- 3 tablespoon lemon juice
- Mustard
- Icing sugar
- Salt
- Black pepper

Preparation:

Mix three egg yolks with lemon juice. Mix olive oil with some sugar and keep stirring it until it becomes dense. Season this sauce with salt, powdered sugar, black pepper and mustard. It's great for cold fish and eggs.

2 Tartar sauce

Ingredients:

- 0,5 dl cream
- 1,5 dl white wine
- Cayenne black pepper
- Salt
- Icing sugar
- Lemon juice
- Mustard

Preparation:

Mix the mayonnaise with white wine and sour cream and mix it with some icing sugar, salt, lemon juice, mustard, cayenne black pepper. Perfect for cold fish, eggs and salads.

3 Remoulade sauce

Ingredients:

- 3 egg yolks
- 0,5 l oil
- Caper berries
- 1 chive
- 1 onion

- 1 parsley
- Tarragon leaf
- Black pepper
- 6-8 vinegar cucumber
- 0,2 l cream
- Salt

Preparation:

Mix the mayonnaise sauce with mustard, black pepper, sliced vinegar cucumbers, onion, parsley and caper berries, then add some cream. Great for cold meals.

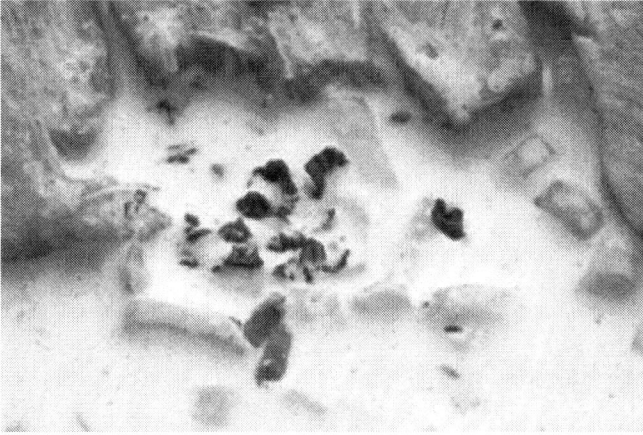

4 Cream sauce

Ingredients:

- Mayonnaise sauce
- Lemon juice
- Cream

Preparation:

Season the mayonnaise sauce with salt and lemon juice. Add some cream, it's great for cold fish meals and snails.

5 Green sauce

Ingredients:

- Mayonnaise sauce
- 1 pack of spinach
- Salt
- 1 pack of chives
- White wine
- Cream

Preparation:

Boil the spinach, then grind it and cool it down. Mix it with mayonnaise, salt, sliced chives. Add some white wine and cream. The sauce should be light green. Great for cold fish and eggs.

6 Tyrol sauce

Ingredients:

- Mayonnaise sauce

- Tomato puree
- Ketchup
- White wine
- Salt
- Sugar
- Cream
- White pepper

Preparation:

Mix the mayonnaise sauce with tomato puree, ketchup, then add some white wine, cream, salt, icing sugar and white wine. Great for cold meats.

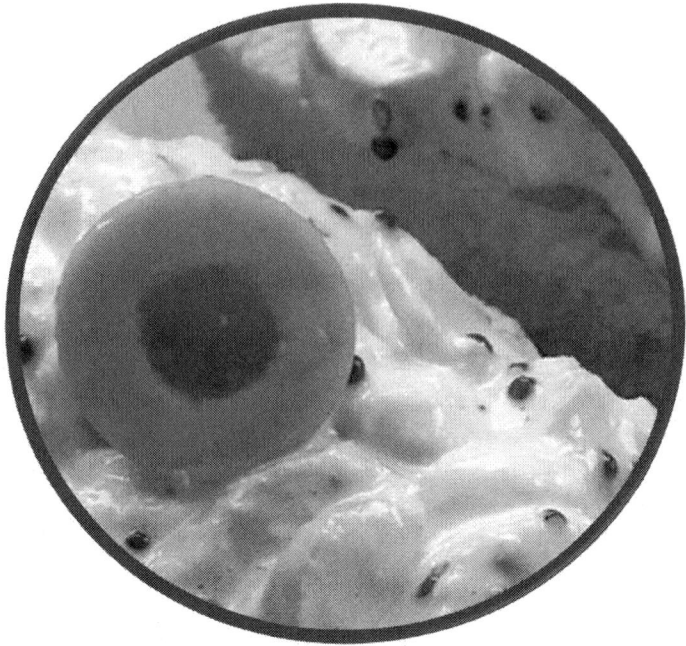

7 Moscow sauce

Prepare a thick, dense tartar sauce and mix it with caviar.

Great for cold fish meals and eggs.

8 Gibice sauce

Ingredients:

- Mayonnaise sauce
- Boiled eggs
- Vinegar cucumber

- Chives
- Parsley
- Tarragon leaf
- Caper berry
- Salt

Preparation:

Mix the mayonnaise sauce with salt, sliced boiled eggs, vinegar cucumbers, chives, tarragon leaves, parsley and caper berries. Great for cold meats, marrow and fish.

9 Swedish sauce

Ingredients:

- Mayonnaise sauce
- Grated apple
- Grated horseradish
- Salt

- Icing sugar
- Lemon juice

Preparation:

Mix the mayonnaise sauce with apple, grated horseradish, salt, icing sugar, lemon juice. Great for cold meats.

10 Csiki sauce

Ingredients:

- Tartar sauce
- Apple
- Boiled beetroot
- Mushroom
- Chives

Preparation:

Peel the apples, then slice up the apples, beetroot and the cooked mushrooms into cubes. Mix it with the tartar sauce and add some chives. Great for meats.

11 Chives sauce

Ingredients:

- Mayonnaise sauce
- Milk
- Bread roll

- Boiled egg yolks
- Salt
- Black pepper
- Lemon juice
- Sour cream
- Chives

Preparation:

Soak the bread roll in milk, twist it, then mix it with mayonnaise sauce. Add some salt to the egg yolks, then some black pepper, lemon juice, add

the cream and the chives. Great for hot and cold beef.

12 Green chaud-froid sauce

Ingredients:

- 0.5 l mayonnaise sauce
- 600 grams aspic
- Lemon
- Icing sugar
- Salt
- Spinach

Preparation:

Boil the spinach then grind it and cool it. Mix the mayonnaise sauce with the cold spinach and the melted, but frozen aspic. It's great for cold fish and egg meals.

Mix it with gelatin if warm, and aspic if it's cold. This way, the top will 'freeze' so you can decorate it with pastel colors.

13 Apple horseradish sauce

Ingredients:

- 1 vinegar horseradish
- 2,5 dl cream
- 4 apples
- Salt
- Sugar

Preparation:

Mix the grated apples, horseradish with cream, and add some salt and icing sugar. Cool it down in the fridge. Great for meats.

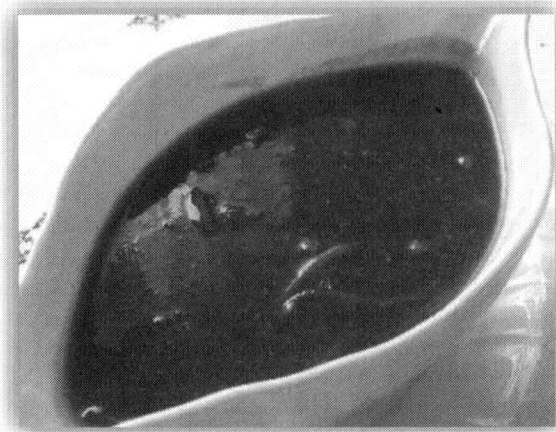

14 Cumberland sauce

Ingredients:

- 250 g blueberry jam
- 2 lemon
- 2 orange
- 1,5 dl red wine
- Mustard
- Black pepper

Preparation:

Peel the oranges and take its juice. Soak the orange peels in red wine for 20 minutes, then add the orange juice, mix it with the blueberry jam.

Season it with the lemon juice, mustard and black pepper. Cool it down and serve it with cold meals.

15 Dutch sauce

Ingredients:

- 4 egg yolks
- 1,5 dl cream
- 1 tablespoon of lemon juice
- 200 g butter
- Salt

- Black pepper (cayenne)

Preparation:

Melt the butter, then mix some egg yolks with cream. Boil water, add the melted butter, and then add some lemon juice, salt, black pepper.

16 Curry sauce

Ingredients:

- half a tube of mayonnaise

- 2 dl yoghurt
- 1 tablespoon lemon juice
- Sugar
- Salt
- Ground black pepper
- Curry dust

Preparation:

Mix the ingredients with an egg-beater or a machine and store it in the fridge.

Great for meats, fish and fried cheese.

White sauce belongs to warm sauces, so why is it here? It's important to know this white basic sauce since this is the base for many cold sauces.

If you don't want store-bought sauces and mayonnaise, then you can make it yourself. Good quality, delicious sauces bring out the best in meals.

Let's check out the white sauce, which is the base for many other sauces.

17 White sauce

Ingredients:

- 50 g butter
- 5 dl broth
- 4 tablespoon fine flour
- Salt
- Ground white pepper

Preparation:

Make a light fry from butter and flour. Add some broth and whip it, then cook for 20-25 minutes on a small fire. This is good for other sauces. The following sauces use the white sauce as a base.

18 Malta sauce

Ingredients:

- 1 dl white sauce
- 1 dl orange juice
- 1 egg yolk
- 20 g butter
- 1 tablespoon lemon juice
- Grated orange peel
- 1 spoon of cream
- Sugar
- Salt

Preparation:

Mix the egg yolk with butter and the other ingredients

19 Mustard sauce

Ingredients:

- half a tube of mayonnaise
- 1 tablespoon mustard
- 1 dl cream
- Salt
- Icing sugar
- 1 tablespoon vinegar horseradish

Preparation:

Mix the ingredients together with an eggbeater or a machine, store it in the fridge and add the horseradish.

Great for meats.

20 Tomato sauce with mustard

Ingredients:

- 1 bottle of ketchup
- 2 tablespoon lemon juice
- 1 pack of parsley
- 2 tablespoon mustard

- 1 medium onion
- 1 dl wine
- Tarragon leaf
- Ground black pepper

Preparation:

Slice the onion, parsley, tarragon. Mix it with wine, add some black pepper, ketchup, mustard, tarragon, lemon juice and ground black pepper. You can serve it hot or cold, great for meats and salads.

21 Dutch sauce

Ingredients:

- 3 egg yolks,
- 1 dl cream,
- 1 tablespoon lemon juice
- 150 g butter
- Salt
- Black pepper

Preparation:

Melt the butter. Mix egg yolks with cream, then add the melted butter and whip it.

Season with salt, black pepper and lemon juice.

22 Charon sauce

Ingredients:

- 1 Dutch sauce
- 2 tablespoon tomato puree

Preparation:

Mix the ingredients.

Great for meat and fish.

23 Csiki sauce

Ingredients:

- 100 g mushroom

- 1 onion
- 1 apple(idared)
- 300 g vinegar beetroot
- 1 tablespoon lemon juice
- 150 g mayonnaise
- 1,5 dl cream
- Salt
- Ground black pepper
- 1 tablespoon horseradish
- 1 tablespoon sugar

Preparation:

Cut the clean mushroom into small cubes, boil for 10 minutes in a bowl of water with some salt and lemon juice. Slice up the onion and the apple into cubes and add it to the bowl. Filter the water from the mushroom, let it cool down and add to the sauce. Mix it well with a mixer. Put it in the fridge for an hour, season it as you like.

Good for meats.

24 Spring sauce

Ingredients:

- 2,5 dl white sauce
- 100 g mayonnaise
- 2 tablespoon of cream
- 1 lemon
- Parsley
- Chives

- 1 vinegar cucumber
- 1 spoon of tomato puree
- Sugar
- Salt
- Black pepper

Preparation:

Cut the chives, parsley and the cucumber into small cubes. Mix it with some white sauce, mayonnaise, cream, tomato puree and add the vegetables.

Season with lemon, salt and black pepper. Great for fish and egg meals.

25 Vinaigrette sauce

Ingredients:

- 0.5 dl oil
- 0,5 dl lemon juice
- 2 hard boiled eggs
- Salt
- Black pepper
- 1 sour cucumber
- 8 caper berries
- Tarragon
- Chives
- 1 dl cream

Preparation:

Slice up the boiled eggs, mix it with oil, lemon juice and cream. Slice the chives, caper berries, tarragon, cucumbers and mix them together. Season with salt, black pepper.

It's great for cold meals.

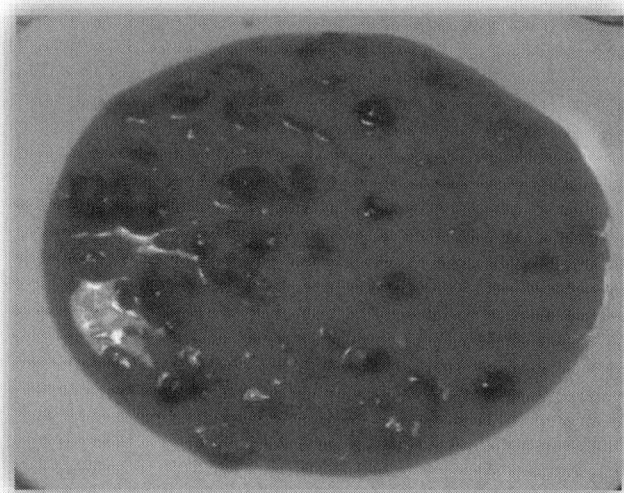

1 Sour cherry sauce

Ingredients:

- 1 l water
- 800 g sour cherry
- 150 g sugar
- 100 g flour
- 2 dl cream
- half lemon
- Ground cinnamon
- Clove
- Salt

Preparation:

Twist the lemon. Mix the water with cinnamon, clove, sugar, salt and lemon peel, boil it, then add the seedless sour cherries, boil for 5 minutes. Mix the cream with flour.

Mix it with the cherries. Boil for another 5 minutes, add some lemon juice and sugar.

You can serve this hot or cold, it's great for meats. Enjoy your meal!

2 Apple sauce

Ingredients:

- 1 kg apple
- 2 dl cream
- 30 g flour
- Spices
- 150 g sugar

Preparation:

Peel the apples and slice them. Boil some water with a bit of salt, sugar and lemon juice, once boiling, add the clean apples and boil until they're soft. Mix some cream with flour, then mix it together, and boil for 3-5 minutes. Add some lemon, sugar. Great hot or cold!

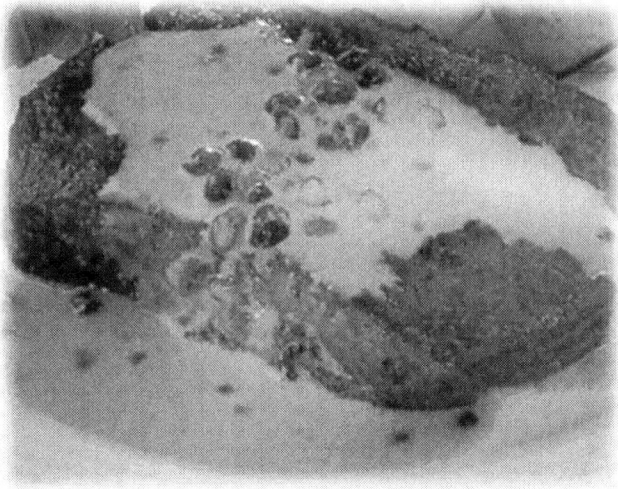

3 Black pepper sauce

Ingredients:

- 1 kg gamey meat
- 500 g bacon
- 4 leek
- 4 onion
- 2 carrot
- Ground white pepper
- Bay leaves
- Nutmeg
- Vinegar
- 5 dl Wine
- Salt
- Butter

Preparation:

Boil the leek in butter, slice up the onion, carrot, and add the ground nutmeg, bay leaves, gamey meat cut into cubes and the raw, smoked bacon.

Boil some ground white pepper in vinegar, then pour it onto the meat. Add the red wine, boil until the meat becomes tender. Once done, filter it. Great for gamey meat.

4 Dill sauce

Ingredients:

- 50 g fat
- 40 g flour
- 3 tablespoon of sliced dill
- 1,5 dl cream
- 2,5 dl broth
- Salt
- 1 small onion
- Sugar

Preparation:

Make some light brown frying base, add the onion cut into cubes and half of the dill, boil it, and add some broth. Boil it while stirring. Add some salt, boil for 15 minutes, and keep stirring. Add the rest of the dill and some cream, boil for 3-5 minutes while stirring. Great for cooked beef.

5 Carrot sauce

Ingredients:

- 600 g carrot

- Flour
- Fat
- 2 tablespoon sugar
- 4 tablespoon vinegar
- Salt

Preparation:

Peel the carrot, slice it up, and boil in salted water until tender.

Mix the sugar, fat and the flour, add the vinegar and the same amount of water.

Boil it well, then add the tender carrots. Boil for one more minute and serve while hot.

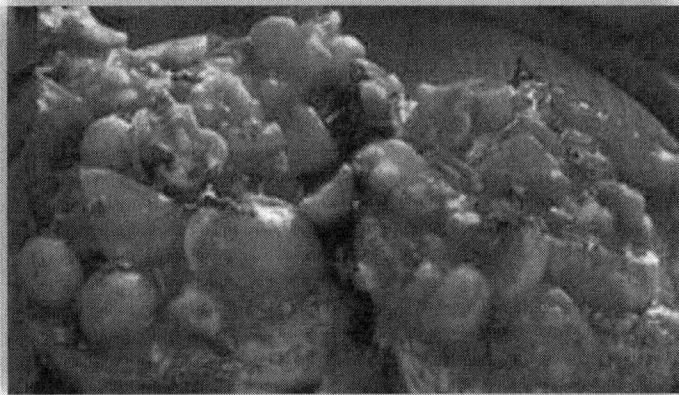

6 Provance sauce

Ingredients:

- 2 dl brown sauce
- 2 tomato
- 1 clove of garlic
- 40 g butter
- 1 dl white wine
- 1 tablespoon of grated garlic
- 70 g mushroom
- Black pepper
- Salt

Preparation:

Boil the brown sauce with wine. Slice up the onion and the mushroom, cook it in butter, add the pressed garlic, tomatoes, salt, black pepper, and cook for 3-5 minutes. Keep stirring, then add the brown wine sauce, add a bit of butter and mix it together.

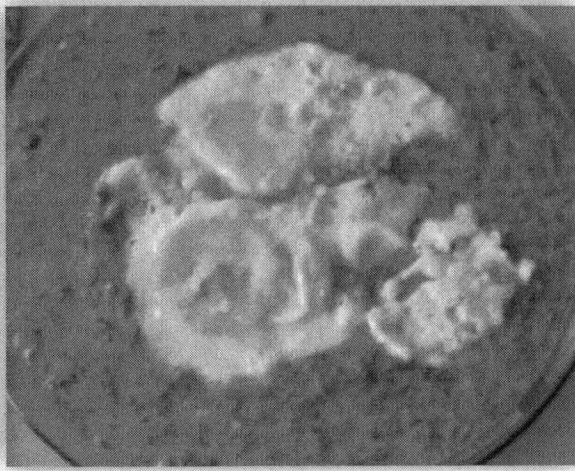

7 Sorrel sauce

Ingredients:

- 600 g sorrel
- Fat
- Flour
- 2,5 dl cream
- Salt
- Sugar

Preparation:

Clean the sorrel and slice it up, cook it on fat, then boil it.

Add some flour and a bit of water, then some salt and sugar.

Boil until it becomes dense, then keep pouring cream while stirring. Boil once again. Great for meats.

8 Vegetable sauce

Ingredients:

- 500 g mixed vegetables
- Carrot
- White carrot
- Peas
- Green bean
- Cauliflower
- Kohlrabi
- Celery
- Parsley
- 60 g butter
- 2 dl yoghurt
- 50 g flour
- 1 dl milk
- Salt

Preparation:

Boil the vegetables in salted water until they become tender.

Prepare a light fry from butter and flour, add some milk and the water from the vegetables.

Add the yoghurt, then season with salt and a bit of sugar. Add the vegetables.

Great for meats.

9 Mushroom sauce

Ingredients:

- 300 g mushroom
- Parsley
- 1 onion
- 1 tablespoon flour
- 2,5 dl cream
- Black pepper
- Salt

Preparation:

Clean the mushroom, slice it up and cook it in fat. Add the finely cut parsley, onion, salt, black pepper. Once tender, add flour, cook for a while, then add water and boil for 1-3 minutes. Serve with sour cream.

10 Hungarian sauce

Ingredients:

- 100 g smoked bacon
- 2 onion
- 1 tablespoon red pepper
- 1.5 dl gravy
- 2,5 dl cream

Preparation:

Cook the finely sliced bacon, then the onion in the fat, add the red pepper, gravy and cream, boil for 2 minutes.
Don't add too much salt! Smoked bacon is salty in itself, so don't salt the gravy either.

11 Sausage sauce

Ingredients:

- 250 g smoked sausage
- 2 small onions
- 2 bay leaves
- 3 tablespoon of flour
- 4 tablespoon of cream

Preparation:

Slice up the sausage into circles, add the sliced up onion, pour some water and add the bay leaves, boil until they become tender. Mix together the cream and the flour, pour it into the bowl, and then boil them together. Good for thick soups or for bread instead of butter.

.

12 Metaxa sauce

Ingredients:

- 3,5 dl water
- 70 g flour
- 3 glass of cream
- 5 cl Metaxa
- 1 bouillon cube
- Black pepper

Preparation:

Put the bouillon cube into water and boil it. Add some flour and cream. Boil, then season with black pepper, then add the Metaxas.

13 Provanse sauce

Ingredients:

- 4 tomatoes
- 1 onion
- 1 clove of garlic
- 2 tablespoon of oil
- Ketchup
- Thyme
- Rosemary
- Salt
- White pepper

Preparation:

Make some cuts into the tomatoes, boil for a few minutes, peel them and dice them into cubes. Clean the onion and the clove of garlic and dice them as well. Heat some oil, add the onion and the garlic. Then add the tomato, ketchup and some sauces, cook for another minute and a half. Finally season with salt and white pepper.

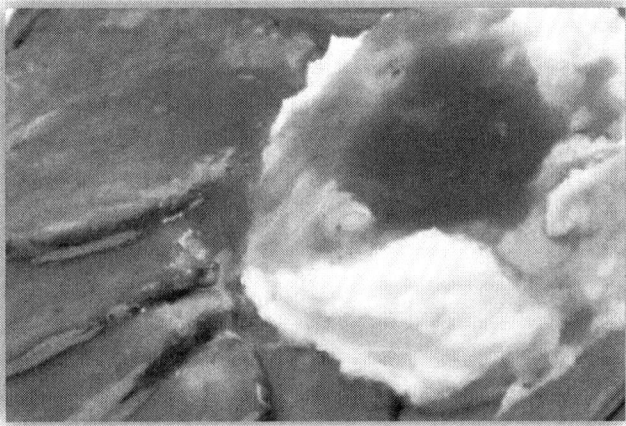

14 Madeira sauce

Ingredients:

- 100 g mixed vegetables

- 1 smoked bacon
- 4 small mushrooms
- 2 tablespoon of flour
- Tomato puree
- Black pepper
- Salt
- Clove
- Sugar
- 1 dl red wine

Preparation:

Toast the vegetables with some sugar, add the diced smoked sausage, then the mushroom, then the flour.

Add the tomato puree and toast until they become tender. Let it cool once done.

Filter this mixture, then reheat again, and add salt, black pepper, clove, sugar, then red wine and boil until it becomes as dense as honey.

Use Madeira wine if you can, but any red wine will do. Great for beef.

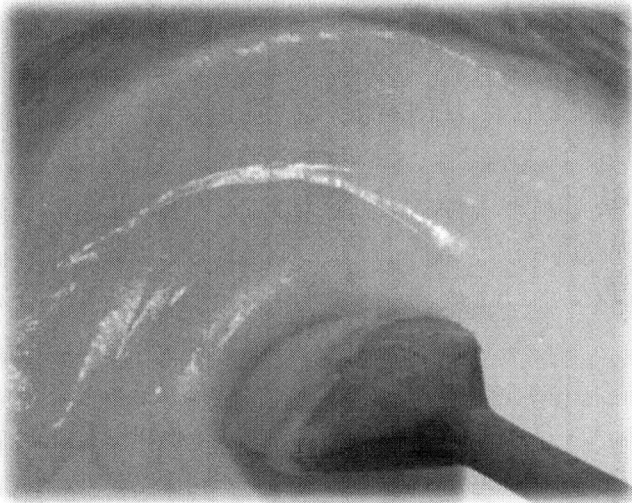

15 Béchamel sauce

Ingredients:

- 1 tablespoon of butter
- 1 tablespoon of flour
- 3 dl milk

- Salt
- Black pepper

Preparation:

This sauce can be used for more things, it's also a base for my next sauce, and however, it's great for casino eggs. Boil the butter, add the flour and make frying material. Boil the milk, pour it together while stirring, once done, season with salt and black pepper. Great for cold meals, such as ham with horseradish.

Mustard and eggs béchamel sauce:

Mix the béchamel sauce with 2 boiled egg yolks and two coffee spoons of mustard.

Cheese béchamel sauce:

Add grated cheese to the béchamel sauce.

Milk-free béchamel sauce:

Replace the milk with broth or fish soup.

Onion béchamel sauce:

Add finely sliced onion, coriander and cream.

16 Spicy sauce

Ingredients:

- 2 dl béchamel sauce
- Chives
- Dill

- Parsley
- 1 tablespoon of butter
- Lemon juice
- Thyme
- Marjoram

Preparation:

Finely slice the chives, thyme, dill, parsley, then add some marjoram and boil it in one tablespoon of butter. Add the pre made béchamel and season with a bit of lemon juice

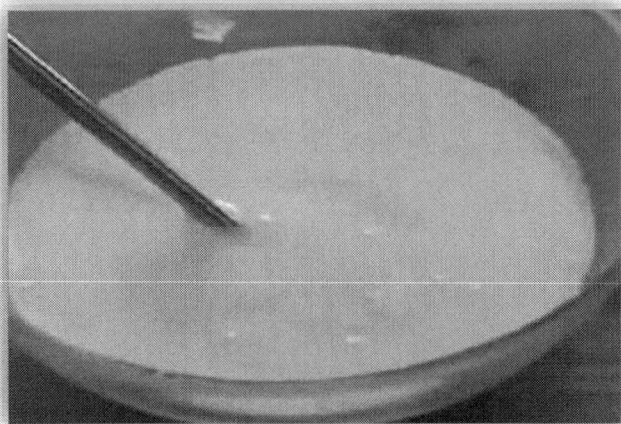

17 Horseradish sauce

Ingredients:

- 200 g horseradish
- 50 g flour
- 3 dl cream
- 50 g sugar
- 50 g fat
- 6 dl broth
- Salt
- Vinegar

Preparation:

Clean the horseradish, grate it onto a plate. Steam it for 3-5 minutes.

Mix together some fat, flour and add some broth to it.

Boil it, add salt. Add the horseradish, then some vinegar, sugar and some salt if needed, then add the cream and boil once again.

It's great for meats.

18 Sour cream and cheese sauce

Ingredients:

- 30 g butter
- 30 g flour
- 2 dl milk

- 2 dl cream
- 70 g cheese
- Salt
- Black pepper
- Nutmeg
- 2 egg yolks

Preparation:

Mix some butter and flour, add some milk, and whip it well. Add salt, black pepper, nutmeg.

Add 1 dl of cream, 70 g of grated cheese and cook for 10 minutes.

Mix the egg yolks with some cream, put it in the sauce, whip it and boil it.

19 Sardine sauce

Ingredients:

- 1 onion
- 1 tablespoon of oil
- 2,5 dl water
- 2,5 dl roast sauce
- 2 washed sardines

Preparation:

Toast the diced onion in some oil, add some water, then some sardines. Great for fish and eggs.

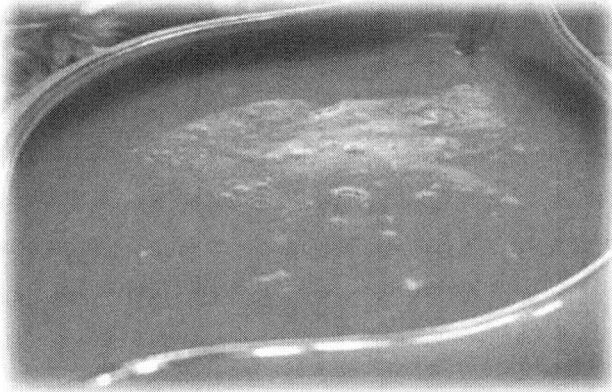

20 Parade sauce

Ingredients:

- 1,5 orange peel

- 1 dl white wine
- 100 g mayonnaise
- 1 small spoon of mustard
- 1 tablespoon of peach jam
- Salt
- Icing sugar

Preparation:

Boil the orange peel in some water, add some juice, wine, mustard, jam, mayonnaise and boil for 5 minutes.

Then add the orange peel and boil for one more minute.

Great for duck and goose.

21 Black pepper sauce

Ingredients:

- 1 teaspoon of black pepper (ground)
- 50 g margarine
- 0.5 tablespoon of flour
- Spice pepper
- 2 dl milk
- Salt
- Nutmeg

- Garlic dust
- Bouillon cube

Preparation:

Melt the margarine, and toast the black pepper. Add some flour and red pepper, then 2 dl of milk. Add the other seasonings. Boil while stirring, wait until it becomes dense. Great for meats, such as turkey in bacon or chicken breast.

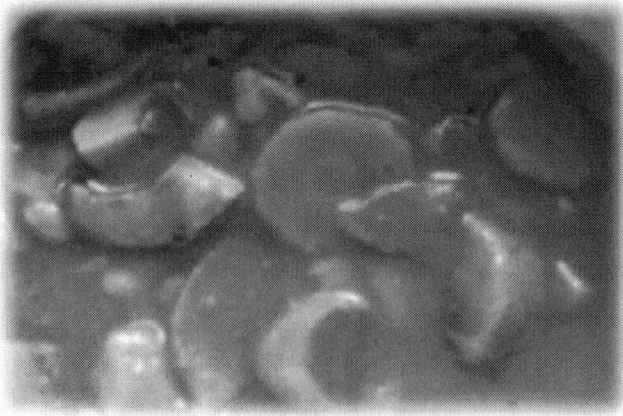

22 Chakala sauce

Ingredients:

- 0,5 dl sunflower oil
- 1 green pepper
- 1 medium onion
- 2 cloves of garlic
- 2 chili pepper
- 1 tablespoon curry dust
- 4 carrots
- 1 medium cauliflower
- 400 g bean tomato can
- Salt
- Black pepper
- 2 big mushrooms
- 50 g sweet pea

Preparation:

Dice the onion, green pepper, and chili, mushroom, slice up the carrot, then wash the cauliflower. Heat up the oil and toast the onion, garlic, chili, curry dust for 5 minutes.

Add the carrot, cauliflower, green peas and the mushroom.

Cook carefully for 10-15 minutes or until the vegetables are done.

Add the bean can and the seasonings. Let it cool down. Serve when cold for meats.

23 Bread roll sauce with chicken

Ingredients:

- 5 bread rolls
- 2 cloves of garlic

- 1 tablespoon of oil
- 1 l chicken broth
- 1200 g chicken meat

Preparation:

Boil the broth for the base of the sauce. Toast some diced bread rolls on a bit of oil, when they become colorful, add the pressed garlic.

Then pour broth onto it. Stir while the bread rolls are still intact.

We recommend that you'd make it fresh. Serve with chicken or any other meat.

24 Horseradish sauce with orange

Ingredients:

- 300 g apple
- 80 g horseradish
- 2 oranges
- 1 lemon
- 1 teaspoon sugar

Preparation:

Grate the peel of the orange and the lemon, twist it, peel the apples and grate them down, then add the horseradish, mix it together with the orange and lemon juice and peel, then add some sugar. Serve it when cold, it's great for all kinds of meat.

25 Dill sauce with sour cream

Ingredients:

- 1 pack of dill
- 1 tablespoon of oil
- 2 dl cream
- 5 tablespoon of flour
- Salt

Preparation:

Wash the dill and slice it into small pieces, cook on some oil, add some water, salt and boil for a bit.

Mix it with cream and flour. Boil them together. Great for meats.

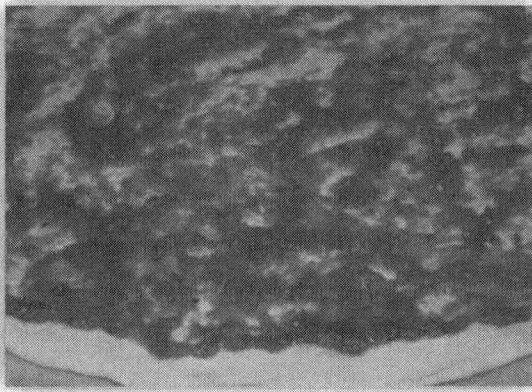

26 Pizza sauce

Ingredients:

- Olive oil

- 6 tomatoes
- 1 onion
- 3 cloves of garlic
- Oregano
- Black pepper
- Salt

Preparation:

Dice the onion, press the garlic and toast them in olive oil. Peel the tomatoes, dice them and mix it together.

Season with black pepper, salt and cook until it becomes dense and thick.

Then add the oregano and boil for about two more minutes.

BOOK 4
Salads, Pasta salads
&
Sweet pastas

Foreword

I would like to highlight that this book is about cooking at home. This is not about restaurant wonders where the customers are enchanted with beautiful-looking dishes.

This book has no wonders or over the top decorations, waiters and so on. This book is about our own kitchen and regular kitchen ingredients.

This book is about our own two hands, hearts and everyday cooking.

Recognition will come from our family, relatives, friends and guests, but more importantly, we must be able to create something that is good.

What is this recognition, you may ask? Simple; 'Thank you! It was delicious!' and so on. However, the best recognition is when all the food is gone. My goal with this and my previous books / "Hungarian cuisine - Main dishes" / /"Hungarian cuisine - Cookbook for beginners - Hungarian soups/ /Hungarian cuisine - Cookbook for beginners - Cold & Hot sauces/

Is to give you my recipes so that you can get this kind of recognition as well.

Book description

Salads are part of every diet, and if we eat it for dinner, we are one step closer to our goal. There are various ways of making salads so we'll never get bored. The best one is the green salad with some vinegar and sugar; this is great for pastas, like egg noodles. It's a myth that you need to avoid fat during a diet, because avoiding it could actually cause harm. Avocadoes are full of good fats that are good for our skin. You can combine green salads, spinach with fruits. These make a great side dish for meats. Eating fish is not very common in Hungary, but sometimes we eat carp, catfish and bream. Shrimps are great, especially if you cook it in olive oil then mix it in a salad. But you can also grill it. Greek salad is also a great choice, you can make it from cucumber, pepper, tomatoes, salad leaves, lemon, olive, and onion and feta cheese, season it with Mediterranean spices and some olive oil and oregano, and it's done.

And the perfect light dinner is ready. Let's talk some more about olive oil. The fatty acids found in it helps weight loss and is good for the heart. You can mix it with balsam vinegar, but it's a great dressing in itself. It's almost a base ingredient for every salad.

1 Lettuce salad

Ingredients:

- 2 Lettuce salad
- 2 tablespoon vinegar 10%
- Salt
- Sugar
- Water 1l

Preparing:

Wash the salad in water, and filter it down. Cut it into 4 pieces, put it in a bowl of cool lettuce juice and serve it on a cool glass bowl.

You can prepare the lettuce juice however you want.

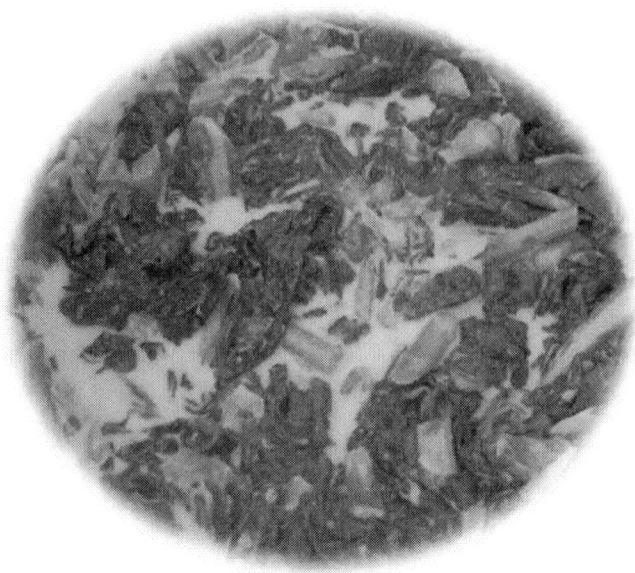

2 Boiled salad

Ingredients:

- 1,5 l lettuce juice
- 5 cloves of garlic
- 100 g smoked bacon
- 3 Lettuce salad

Preparing:

Slice the lettuce into stripes, dice the smoked bacon, toast it and filter some pork rind. Add the pressed garlic to the fat and add the lettuce juice. Put the lettuce into it. Serve when hot.

3 Cucumber salad

Ingredients:

- 1500 g fresh cucumber

- 2 tablespoon vinegar
- 200 g Sugar
- Bit of black pepper
- Spice paprika for decoration
- Salt
- 4 cloves of garlic
- 1 l liquid

Preparing:

Peel the cucumbers, add some salt and then wash it. Put it into lettuce juice, season with pressed garlic and once done, put it onto a cooled down salad plate. Add some spice paprika and black pepper.

4 Pepper salad

Ingredients:

- 1,2 Lettuce juice
- Salt
- 1500 g Green pepper

Preparing:

Wash the green pepper and take out its seeds. Slice it into small circles, boil it, pour it down with cold water and put it into cooled down salad vinegar. If the pepper is weak, don't boil it, just add salt, then the vinegar.

5 Tomato salad

Ingredients:

- 3 onions
- 1 Chive
- 1500 g tomato

- Ground black pepper
- Oil
- Salt

Preparing:

Wash the tomato, take out the cob, then peel it and slice it up. Place onto a glass plate, add some onions, chives, black pepper, vinegar and a few drops of oil.

6 Onion salad

Ingredients:

- Oil
- 1,5 Onion
- Ground black pepper

Preparing:

Slice the onion into thin slices. Add some salt, then wash it. Put the onion onto a plate, add some lettuce juice and cool it down. Add some oil to the top, then some black pepper.

7 Cabbage salad

Ingredients:

- Cabbage: 1500 g
- Oil
- Salt
- Sugar
- Cumin

Preparing:

Slice the cabbage into 2 mm wide slices. Add some salt, squeeze out the water, and put it into precooled lettuce juice. Season with cumin. Place onto a pre-cooled glass plate and add some oil.

8 Beetroot salad

Ingredients:

- 1,5 l Lettuce juice
- Vinegar

- Salt
- 2000 g beetroot
- Sugar
- Cumin
- Horseradish

Preparing:

Don't cut out the root of the beetroot else its color will come out during boiling.

Wash the beetroot then boil until tender. Once done, wash it down with cold water and peel it. Slice it up with a wavy edged knife. Put it onto a plate of cool lettuce juice, add horseradish and cumin.

9 Potato salad

Ingredients:

- 1.5 l Lettuce juice
- Vinegar
- Salt
- Black pepper
- 2000 g Potato
- Sugar
- Onion
- Chives

- Oil

Preparing:

Kidney potatoes are recommended. Boil in salted water. Cool it down and slice it up. Put it into a bowl of cool vinegar with onion circles. Serve on a glass plate, add oil, black pepper and chives.

10 Green bean salad

Ingredients:

- 1,2 l Lettuce juice
- Salt
- Vinegar 10%
- Green bean
- Tarragon
- 2 onions
- 5 pickles
- Oil
- Black pepper
- Chives

Preparing:

Boil the green beans in salted water until tender, then cool it down and put it into a bowl of lettuce juice. Put it into a glass plate and decorate with chives.

11 Broccoli salad

Ingredients:

- 1l lettuce juice
- 4 g Salt
- 4 g sugar
- Parsley

- Tarragon
- 1200 g Broccoli
- Caper berries
- 6 pickles
- 1 onion
- Oil
- Black pepper

Preparing:

Wash the broccoli, boil in salted water for a while, once done, cool it down and mix with lettuce juice.

Pasta salads

1 Pasta salad with ham

Delicious salad, great side dish.

Ingredients:

- 200 g pasta
- 5 dl sour cream
- 2 dl kefir
- 150 g mayonnaise (optional)

- 1 tablespoon mustard
- 1 teaspoon of lemon juice
- bit of icing sugar
- Salt
- Black pepper
- 1 teaspoon of hot pepper cream
- 200 g ham
- 200 g cheese
- 300 g sweetcorn
- 3 leek

Preparing:

Mix the mayonnaise, mustard, lemon juice, icing sugar then add the sour cream and kefir, add some salt, black pepper and hot pepper cream.

Add the diced ham and cheese, then the corn and leek and mix it with the pasta. Season, then cool it down.

2 Pasta salad with sausage and corn

A cold salad is great for the family in the summer heat because cooking is hard in extreme heat.

Ingredients:

- 200 g pasta cake
- 350 g smoked Vienna sausage
- 1 onion
- 1 apple
- 140 g sweet corn (1 an)
- 4 tablespoon mayonnaise
- 330 g sour cream
- 150 g yoghurt
- 1 teaspoon mustard
- Salt
- Black pepper
- 1 teaspoon of sugar

Preparing:

Boil the pasta in salted water, wash it down with cold water, and filter it. Slice the onion, apple and Vienna sausage, pour the sweet corn juice onto it, and then add the sweet corn. Mix some mayonnaise with sour cream, yoghurt and mustard. Season with salt, black pepper and a bit of sugar. Mix the ingredients. Cool it down for a few hours, serve when cold.

3 Pasta salad with chicken breast

Fast salad, especially if we have leftover pasta or chicken breast.

Ingredients:

Chicken:

- 400 g chicken breast fillet
- 0.25 dl olive oil
- Salt
- Black pepper
- Thyme

Salad:

- 250 g pasta
- 40 g olives
- 0.25 green Californian pepper
- 150 g goat cheese
- 1 onion
- 100 g cocktail tomatoes
- 50 g dried tomatoes

The sauce:

- 3 dl yoghurt
- 2 tablespoon olive oil
- 1 tablespoon mustard
- Lemon juice
- 4 tablespoon basil
- Black pepper

Preparing:

Dice the chicken breast, add the spices, 0.25 olive oil, salt, black pepper, thyme, mix it well and toast in a pan. Prepare the salad, boil the pasta. Slice up the onion, dried tomato, Californian pepper and the goat cheese.

Once the pasta is ready and not hot, mix it with all the other ingredients. Add the yoghurt, olive oil, mustard, basil, then season with lemon juice and black pepper. Put it in the fridge for an hour.

4 Pasta salad with smoked cheese

This is my wife's specialty and it is liked by everyone. She made these for graduations and guests. This is a great meal for guests because it's a fast and good recipe that's very delicious.

Ingredients:

- 500 g pasta
- 350 g sour cream
- 220 g mayonnaise
- 2 tablespoon mustard
- Salt
- White pepper
- 2 tablespoon basil
- 250 g ham
- 2 onion
- 300 g smoked cheese

Preparing:

Boil the pasta in salted water for 10-15 minutes. Grab a bowl and add some sour cream, mayonnaise, mustard and basil for the sauce. Season as you'd like, with salt and black pepper. Slice up the onion, dice up the ham and the smoked cheese and mix it with mayonnaise and sour cream. Filter the pasta and add it to the sauce. Let it cool for a while and it's ready to be served.

5 Pasta salad with Mediterranean tuna

Cold appetizer, good meal.

Ingredients:

- 250 g colorful durum pasta
- 6 tomatoes
- 2 tablespoon caper berries
- 160 g tuna can
- 3 cobs of corn
- 2 tablespoon olive oil

The sauce:

- 4 tablespoon mayonnaise
- 4 tablespoon yoghurt
- 1 tablespoon lemon juice
- Salt
- Black pepper
- A bit of sugar

Preparing:

Boil the corn, and take them off from the cob. Boil the pasta and add some oil, let it cool. Soak the caper berries in cold water before using it because the berry cans are salty. Mix the sauce. Put them into a bowl in the following order: Pasta, diced tomatoes, caper berries, sauce, tuna and so on.

Cool in the fridge for 2 hours.

6 Pasta salad with tuna and mayonnaise

Delicious tuna salad.

Ingredients:

- 300 g tuna can
- 200 g gnocchi

- 5 tablespoon mayonnaise
- 1 red Californian pepper
- 3 tomato
- 1 onion
- 1 clove of garlic
- 0.5 lemon's juice
- 1 teaspoon of black pepper

Preparing:

Boil the gnocchi in salted water, then pour cold water onto the semi hard pasta.

Toast half an onion and a clove of garlic on some oil. Add a bit of lemon juice and mayonnaise, mix it and season. The sauce is ready. Dice the vegetables, mix them in a bowl with the cooled pasta and the filtered tuna can. Add the sauce and seasoning.

7 Avocado pasta salad

Quick pasta salad for a quick grilled fish.

Ingredients:

- 150 g pasta
- 1 small avocado
- 0,5 lemon's juice
- 1 tablespoon fresh parsley
- 1 tablespoon chives
- 1 tablespoon tarragon
- 1 clove of garlic
- 4 small tomatoes
- 2-3 handfuls of salt

Preparing:

Boil the pasta in hot salted water. Pour cold water onto it, filter it. While boiling, wash the avocado, cut in half, and take out its meat. Add some lemon juice, salt and spices. Slice up the garlic and smash it with your knife. Add this to the avocado, mix it well. Cut the tomatoes in half and mix it alongside the pasta in the avocado sauce.

8 Spaghetti salad

My sister-in-law made this for New Years' Eve, this has been our tradition ever since.

Ingredients:

- 500 g spaghetti pasta
- 1 cucumber
- 200 g diced ham
- 200 g cheese
- 10 tablespoon mayonnaise
- 500 g sour cream
- 2 teaspoon mustard
- Salt
- 2 tablespoon sugar
- 1 tablespoon lemon juice

Preparing:

Boil the spaghetti. Make a sauce from mayonnaise, mustard, sugar, salt, lemon juice and sour cream. Make plenty because the pasta will soak it. I usually make it from one small and one big sour cream. While the pasta is cooling, slice up some ham, cucumber, cheese and mix it with the sauce.

Once the pasta is cooled, mix it with the sauce. Cool it for a few hours.

9 Rich pasta salad

I love this pasta salad, it's a side dish, but also a great main course, especially with some meat. Perfect for guests.

Ingredients:

- 250 g penne
- 450 g sour cream
- 1 tablespoon mayonnaise

- 1 tablespoon ketchup
- 2 tablespoon Dijon mustard
- Oregano
- Black pepper
- Salt
- 1 apple
- 3 radish
- 6 pickle
- 1 leek
- 150 g sweet corn
- 150 g red beans
- 1 tablespoon olive oil
- 200 g grated cheese

Preparing:

Boil the pasta in salted water. Once done, filter it and put it in a bigger bowl, add some olive oil so it doesn't get stuck. While the pasta is cooling, prepare the sauce. Mix sour cream and mayonnaise, then some ketchup, mustard and spices. Peel an apple and dice it alongside the radish, leek and cucumber. Filter the can, add beans and corn.

Add the vegetables, and mix the sauce with the pasta. Cool for a few hours. Add some grated cheese or parsley greens when serving it.

10 Pasta salad with ham, cheese and pumpkin

Great for making this with kids as everybody has something to do.

Ingredients:

- 300 g fusilli pasta
- 200 g pumpkin
- 100 g mozzarella
- 100 g blue cheese
- 50 g ham
- 3 thyme
- Salt
- 1 tablespoon olive oil

Preparing:

Slice up the pumpkin, boil for a few minutes in salted water. Boil the pasta in salted water, add one teaspoon of olive oil. Slice up the cheese and the ham and mix it with the pumpkin and the pasta. Season with thyme and salt.

Mayonnaise salads

1 French salad

Ingredients:

- 550 g mixed vegetables
- 350 g potato
- 150 g vegetable can
- 200 g pickles
- 200 g apple
- Salt
- Mustard
- Tartar sauce

Preparing:

Wash the mixed vegetables, dice them and boil in salted water. Wash the potatoes and boil them and once done, peel and dice them. Dice the pickles as well. Filter the pea can, dice the apples. Add salt and white pepper. Then make some tartar sauce. Season with lemon juice and mustard. Cool for 3 hours, it's great for cold meats!

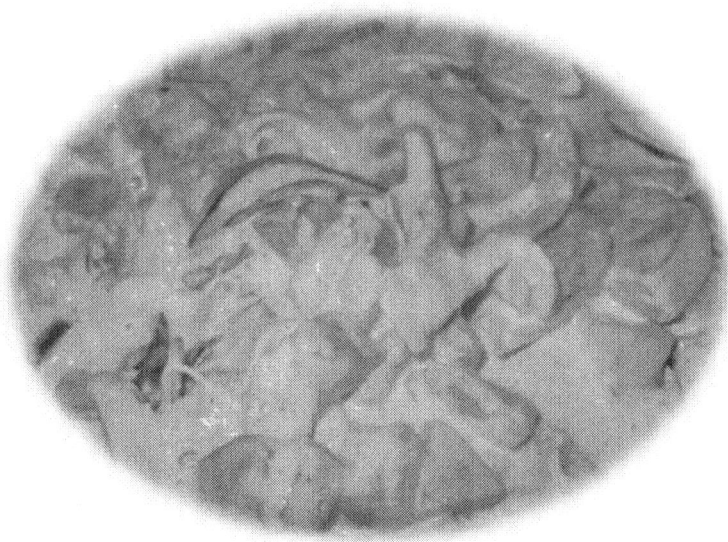

2 Mayonnaise potato salad

Ingredients:

- 1000 g potatoes
- 250 g mayonnaise
- 20 g icing sugar
- 50 g mustard
- Salt
- Lemon
- Ground white pepper
- 300 g ham
- 1 Lettuce salad

Preparing:

Boil the kidney potatoes without peeling them, then cool and slice them into 3 cm wide pieces. Then mix with some mayonnaise, season it. Store in fridge until served.

3 Russian meat salad

Ingredients:

- 600 g roast chicken breast
- 200 g potatoes
- 150 g apple
- 150 g pickles
- Mustard
- Salt
- 20 g icing sugar
- 10 g mayonnaise

Preparing:

Boil the roast chicken breast, apple, pickles, potatoes and slice them up. Mix with seasoned mayonnaise. Store in fridge.

4 Mayonnaise mushroom salad

Ingredients:

- 1000 g Champion mushroom
- 200 g mayonnaise
- Lemon
- Icing sugar
- Ground white pepper
- Salt
- Mustard

Preparing:

Wash the mushrooms and boil in salted water with lemon. Once cooled, slice it up and mix with mayonnaise, then store in the fridge. Serve with parsley.

5 Mayonnaise cauliflower salad

Ingredients:

- 1000 g washed cauliflower
- 2 dl tartar sauce
- 2dl mayonnaise
- 20 g salt
- 20 g ham
- 1 parsley greens

Preparing:

Wash the cauliflower and boil it in salted water, let it cool and filter it down. Put the tartar sauce in a pre-cooled glass bowl and mix the cauliflower. Serve with ham and parsley greens.

6 Mayonnaise herring salad

Ingredients:

- 100 g steamed herring

- 300 g mayonnaise
- 50 g icing sugar
- Lemon
- 1 egg
- 1 lettuce

Preparing:

Take out the marinated herring's spine, cut down its tail and fins. Slice it up into stripes. Put it in a bowl, add seasoned mayonnaise and mix it. Decorate with herring slices.

7 Mayonnaise mixed salad

Ingredients:

- 4 Lettuce salad
- 350 g Tomato salad
- 300 g mayonnaise
- 1 dl cream

- Lemon
- Salt
- Icing sugar
- Ground white pepper
- Parsley greens

Preparing:

Put the mayonnaise in a bowl and mix with cream and spices, add the tomato salad and the sliced lettuce. Store in fridge, decorate with parsley greens when serving.

8 Mayonnaise green bean salad

Ingredients:

- 800 g green bean
- Salt
- 10 dl lemon juice
- 250 g mayonnaise
- Icing sugar
- Ground white pepper
- Parsley greens

Preparing:

Boil the washed green beans in salted water. Slice into 2 cm wide pieces. Once cooled, mix with mayonnaise. Store in fridge and decorate with parsley greens when serving.

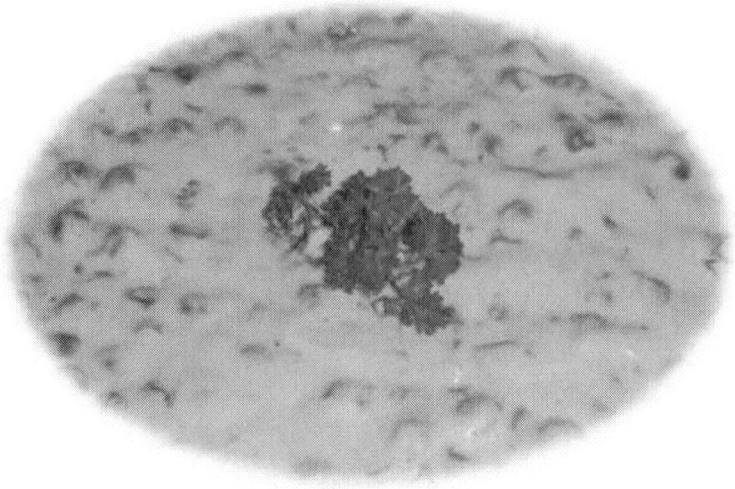

9 Mayonnaise pea salad

Ingredients:

- 750 g green peas
- 350 g mayonnaise
- 30 g icing sugar
- 1 lemon
- Parsley greens
- Salt

Preparing:

Wash the green peas, boil it. Add salt and boil until tender. Filter it, let it cool. Mix mayonnaise with icing sugar, lemon juice and add the peas. Store in fridge for 2 hours. Serve in a cool glass plate, decorate with parsley greens. Great for roast meats.

10 Pasta salad with yoghurt

Ingredients:

- 200 g pasta
- 150 g ham
- 1 corn can
- half cucumber
- 2 dl yoghurt
- 0,5 dl olive oil
- 2 cloves of garlic
- Basil
- Chives
- Salt
- Black pepper
- Lemon juice

Preparing:

Boil the pasta. While boiling, mix the yoghurt, olive oil, pressed garlic and the chives. Add salt, black pepper and a bit of lemon juice. Dice the ham and the cucumber. Pour down the corn's juice, filter the pasta, mix with a bit of olive oil, and let it cool afterwards. Mix with the vegetables, add yoghurt

sauce on top. You can use other vegetables as well.

11 Pasta salad with chicken

Ingredients:

- 350 g short macaroni
- 300 g zucchini
- 2 chicken breast fillet
- 2 cloves of garlic
- 2 tablespoons of mustard
- 2 dl cream
- Salt
- Oil
- Nutmeg
- Parmesan

Preparing:

Boil the pasta in salted water.

While the pasta is boiling, heat up some oil and fry the diced chicken breast fillet. Once almost ready, add the sliced up zucchini and the pressed garlic. Mix mustard with cream, nutmeg, add it to the meat and fry them together, but not for long. Filter the pasta, add it to the mix, add some salt. Serve with grated parmesan.

12 Sweet potato salad with chicken

Ingredients:

- 500 g sweet potatoes
- 400 g chicken breast
- 100 g kale or spinach
- 2 tablespoons of olive oil
- 2 cloves of garlic
- Salt
- Black pepper

Preparing:

Wash the chicken breast, dice them. Toast on a bit of olive oil, add some salt, black pepper and add the pressed garlic. Peel some sweet potatoes and slice them up. Put them in a bowl, add some olive oil and cook on 180 degrees for 25-30 minutes. Meanwhile, steam some spinach or kale. Once the potato is almost tender, add the chicken breast and the spinach or kale. Season it. Cook together for 10 minutes.

Sweet pastas

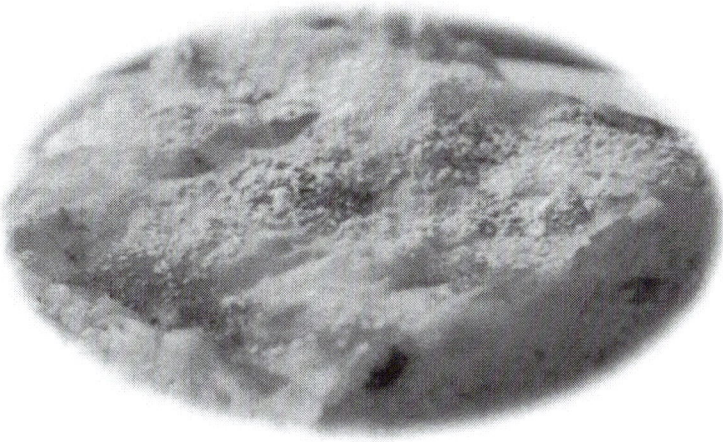

1 Sweet noodle cake

Ingredients:

- 1kg cottage cheese
- 200 g butter
- 7 egg
- Strudel pasta
- 1 pack of pasta
- Bit of fat, or butter
- 300 g sugar
- 3dl sour cream
- 100 g raisins
- Vanilla
- Lemon peel

Preparing:

Mix the butter, sugar, egg yolks and sour cream. Add the cottage cheese, raisins, vanilla icing sugar and a bit of lemon peel. Boil the pasta in salted water, cool it down and mix it with the cottage cheese mix. Whip some egg whites and mix it together. Add butter to a baking sheet, add the strudel pasta and the cottage cheese. Then add another layer like this. Cook in medium heat for 30 minutes.

2 Sweet cake with rice pudding

Ingredients:

- 8 dl milk
- 200 g rice
- Bit of salt
- Vanilla 3 rods
- 30 g butter
- 3db egg
- 120 g icing sugar
- Half lemon peel
- 1.5 liter raspberry syrup

Preparing:

Boil the rice in milk with salt and vanilla, then cool it down, take out the vanilla. Whip it with some butter, sugar and egg yolks, then add some egg whites and cool it down. Add a bit of oil to a baking sheet, then some crumbs, and add the rice. Cook on medium heat. Add raspberry pie in a separate cup.

3 Pasta boiled in milk

Ingredients:

- 400 g flour
- 2 egg
- 1 liter milk
- 60 g butter
- 100 g sugar
- 100 g walnut
- Vanilla sugar
- Salt

Preparing:

Make hard pasta from flour, eggs, make it 1 cm wide. Boil 1 dl of milk, add some salt and vanilla sugar. Boil the pasta in this. Filter it, then mix it with a bit of warm butter. Add the remaining milk. Put in the oven for 10 minutes. Serve with walnut and sugar.

4 Pasta made from wheat meal

Ingredients:

- 1 pack of pasta
- 200 g semolina
- Bit of fat
- Salt

Preparing:

Boil the pasta in salted water, then cool it down. Toast the semolina on a bit of fat. Add the salted water alongside the filtered pasta. Serve with jam and sugar.

5 Cottage cheese dumpling

Ingredients:

- 500 g cottage cheese
- 2 dried bread rolls
- 2 egg
- 200 g breadcrumbs
- Salt
- 1 dl oil
- 20 g butter
- 4 dl sour cream

Preparing:

Dice the bread rolls, dry them in a baking sheet a bit. Mix the cottage cheese with the breadcrumbs, a bit of salt and eggs, let it stand for half an hour. Make balls with a wet hand, boil in salted water. Toast the breadcrumbs on a bit of oil, then add some butter and add the balls. Serve with sour cream, icing sugar.

6 Ham cube

Ingredients:

- 1 pack of wavy pasta
- 3 egg
- 2 dl sour cream
- 200 g ham
- 2 spoons of oil

- 4dkg butter
- 50 g breadcrumbs
- Salt

Preparing:

Boil the pasta in salted water, then cool it down and filter it. Mix 2 egg yolks with warm butter, add the minced ham, sour cream and eggs. Mix it well. Add some butter to a bowl, add breadcrumbs, then the pasta and bake for 25 minutes in the oven.

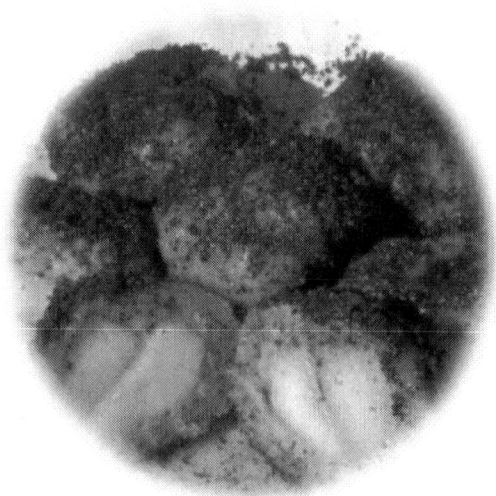

7 Poppy seed dumpling

Ingredients:

- 150 g poppy seed
- 3 bread roll
- 4 dl milk
- 4 egg
- 4 teaspoons of semolina
- Salt
- 50 g butter

Preparing:

Slice up the dried bread rolls into small slices, mix with poppy seeds, and add some hot milk. Once the bread rolls have soaked the milk, mix them together with some eggs, semolina, bit of salt and make egg sized balls. Boil for 10 minutes in boiling water. Filter it, then add diced white bread slices, serve with jam or compote.

8 Meaty bag

Ingredients:

- 300 g flour
- 4 egg
- 150 g beef
- 150 g veal
- 100 g veal marrow

- 20 g spinach
- 1 onion
- 100 g butter
- Bit of ground black pepper
- Nutmeg
- 200 g Grated cheese

Preparing:

Make some pasta from flour, 2 eggs, salt and a bit of water. Put the meats in separate bowls. Put it onto sliced, toasted onion, add some salt, black pepper, and some grated cheese with eggs. Cool it down. Make the pasta round, and put a walnut sized stuffing in the middle. Paste with eggs, fold it. Boil it in hot salted water. Filter it, add it to a bowl with butter and a bit of grated cheese. Add the remaining cheese, put it in a hot oven. Serve with tomato sauce.

9 Strapacka

Ingredients:

- 500 g potatoes
- 1 egg
- Bit of flour
- 100 g butter
- 250 g sheep cottage cheese
- 150 g smoked bacon

Preparing:

Grate the potatoes raw, mix with eggs, salt and enough flour to make it dense as noodles. Paste a bowl with butter. Make noodles from the mixture, add it to the bowl, boil it, filter it, and then add some cottage cheese on top. Put it in the oven so that the cottage cheese gets a bit solid. Add the bacon and hint it with the bacon's fat.

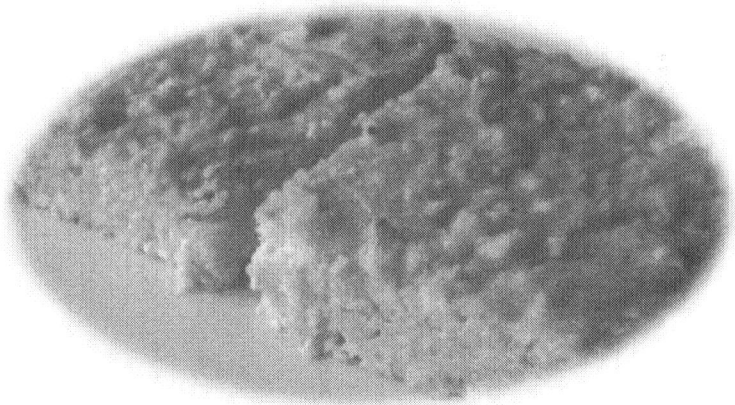

10 Light sweet noodle cake

I've cooked this twice. I saw many recipes, I compared them and decided to make my own.

This is how this light version was born. The family really liked it.

Ingredients:

- 300 g pasta
- 500 g cottage cheese
- 5 egg
- 1 egg yolks
- 50 g raisins
- 1 pack of Strudel pasta
- 1 Lemon peel (grated)
- 1 pack of vanilla sugar
- 150 g icing sugar
- 2 dl sour cream
- 50 g butter
- 1 dl sunflower oil

Preparing:

Boil the pasta in salted water, add a bit of oil, but don't boil for more than 3 minutes. Filter it and mix with butter. Don't let the pasta get soft! Ground the cottage cheese with a fork.

Separate the eggs.

Mix the egg yolks with sugar, add the grated lemon peel, vanilla sugar, raisins and mix with cottage cheese and sour cream.

Whip the egg whites, mix it with the cottage cheese mix.

Add the cooled pasta with the cottage cheese mix.

Paste the baking sheet with oil and strudel pasta, paste with oil, and add another strudel pasta layer, paste with oil, and another layer.

Once done, add the cottage cheese mix pasta so that the top has some oil on it.

Paste the top layer with some oil and egg yolk mixture.

Put it in a pre-heated oven and bake at 200°C for 45 minutes.

11 Pasta with walnut and jam

Variation for pasta and walnut.

Ingredients:

- Pasta:
- 2 eggs

- 200 g fine flour (depending on the size of the eggs)
- The stuffing:
- 4 eggs
- 7 tablespoon icing sugar
- 4 dl sour cream
- 50 g butter
- 100 g ground walnut
- 6 tablespoon fruit jam
- 1 tablespoon breadcrumbs
- Preparing the bowl:
- 1 tablespoon butter

Preparing:

Make pasta from eggs, flour.

Mix egg yolks with 4 tablespoons of icing sugar, mix with butter and sour cream.Whip egg whites with 1 tablespoon of icing sugar.

Boil the pasta in salted water, filter it, mix it with the sour cream mixture, then the egg whip. Preheat the oven to 180C. Put some butter and breadcrumbs into a bowl, then add half of the pasta. Add the icing sugar and walnut mix, then some jam and the remaining pasta. Put it in the oven and bake for 30-35 minutes.

12 Pasta with poppy seeds

Another version of the poppy seed pasta, this is a lot more delicious!

Ingredients:

- 500 g pasta
- 1 tablespoon sunflower oil

- 200 g poppy seed
- 120 g icing sugar
- 1 pack of vanilla sugar
- 3 dl sour cream
- 1 egg
- 250 g peach jam
- 1 tablespoon breadcrumbs
- 40 g butter

Preparing:

Mix the poppy seeds with 100 g of icing sugar. Boil the pasta in salted water, add a bit of oil, and then filter it down once done.

Mix the pasta in a bigger bowl with the poppy seed mixture. Then paste a baking sheet with butter and add the breadcrumbs.

Add half of the pasta, then some peach jam, then the remaining pasta. Mix some sour cream with icing sugar, vanilla sugar and one egg.

Pour it onto the top of the pasta. Put it in a preheated oven at 220C, bake for 25-30 minutes. Serve with icing sugar.

13 Baked pasta with apple and cinnamon

This pasta is great, whether it's salty or sweet!

This sweet version is loved by many in our family.

Ingredients:

- 500 g pasta
- 4 apples
- 150 g peach jam

- 3 eggs
- 2 dl sour cream
- 50 g butter
- 1 teaspoon of cinnamon
- 2 tablespoon of honey
- 1 teaspoon of salt

Preparing:

Boil the pasta in salted water, add some cold water, filter it, and mix with butter. Peel the apples and grate them down. Mix egg yolks with honey, but only use its first half. Add jam to the other half, then cinnamon and the grated apple. Mix it with the pasta and put it onto a baking sheet.

Whip some egg yolks and mix it with sour cream and the other half of the egg yolks, add some sugar too.

Pour it onto the top of the pasta, then put it in a preheated oven and bake at medium heat for about 30-32 minutes. Dice it into cubes when serving it.

14 Tyrol cubes

This is a delicious Austrian specialty.

Ingredients:

- 250 g big cube pasta
- 80 g butter
- 80 g icing sugar
- 20 g vanilla sugar

- 4 eggs
- 2.5 dl sour cream
- 1 handful of raisins
- 1 grated Lemon peel
- 250 g cow cottage cheese
- 1 tablespoon butter
- 2 tablespoon icing sugar

Preparing:

Boil the pasta in salted water, filter it. Whip some butter, icing sugar, vanilla sugar and egg yolks.

7Add some sour cream, grated lemon peel, then some raisins and the whipped eggs.

Mix the pasta with the cottage cheese, then put it into the egg mixture.

Paste a bowl with butter and add some icing sugar. Add the pasta evenly.

Put it in a preheated oven at 180C, bake for 30 minutes. Serve with icing sugar and cut into cubes.

15 Cherry strudel

I like its simplicity and the ingredients are delicious. I prepared and made this. It was better than expected.

Ingredients:

- 300 g strudel pasta
- 300 ml kefir
- 150 g sour cream
- 2 eggs

- 3 packs of vanilla sugar
- 5 tablespoon sugar
- 100 g sour cherry
- 100 g peach jam
- 3 dl milk
- 1 tablespoon butter

Preparing:

Mix the eggs, sugar, vanilla sugar, kefir, sour cream, then add 3 dl of milk while stirring. This mixture should be thin. Paste the baking sheet with some butter, add the strudel pasta evenly.

Add the cherries, then some peach jam, then pour the milk mixture on top. Move the pasta so that the milk is spread out evenly, otherwise it will get dry. Bake in a preheated oven at medium heat until the top starts to get red. Wait for it to cool down, cut it into cubes and serve with icing sugar.

23367628R00190

Printed in Great Britain
by Amazon